From There to Here:

An Insider's Guide

to Navigating the

Darkness

Thank you
Dear Sister,
Laura

—

Rev Rachel A. Hollander

rev rachel

From There to Here: An Insider's Guide to Navigating the Darkness Copyright © 2021 by Rev Rachel Hollander

ISBN (978-0-578-24774-8)

Printed in USA by 48HrBooks (www.48HrBooks.com)

Because of Maddie, Iris and Buddy....
and Jimmy, my lifeline.

Table of Contents

Prologue - From There to Here

Why this book? And why this title?

I have lived with depression - the worst roommate ever - for as long as I can remember. Pretty sure I came into this life with it.

I am writing this book now is because I have finally learned to live *differently* than I used to. With a deeper awareness, better strategies, and a whole lot of Gratitude. I wasn't always like this. Learning to live Gratefully was a lesson that came to me much later in life.

This book came into being because I wanted to support people like me, those who are trying to stay alive and learn to live with depression. I also wanted to support those people who love people like me. To offer some insight into what this journey of navigating the darkness is like. Especially if they have never experienced it themselves.

Getting from "there" to "here" is not a totally accurate assessment of how this all works, though.

The concept of getting from there to here is kind of like a Zen Koan – a riddle or puzzle that can reveal greater truths. Because our "there" is no longer real, it is just a fading memory. And there is no true "here" either. We get to each "here" in each moment that we choose to stay alive.

"Here" is a moving target. And "there" is just a collection of the stories we tell. As a wise person shared once, "Stories are where memories go when they're forgotten."

That is the reason this book exists.

Each of our lives is like one long Camino. A journey. And it's a journey that is filled with smaller journeys - stories - that detail each and every moment we spent getting from there to here, then here, then here, and on and on.

My hope is that I have learned enough from each of my "there" moments that they can sustain me, enhance my experiences, and fill my life with Gratitude that I have made it to yet another "here" moment.

How do we get from there to here?
Start by taking a deep breath.

Introduction

I have traveled the road of mental illness and learned a lot along the way. I am still on it. It has not been a linear journey – an "I was sick and now I'm better" kind of trek. It's definitely more of a "one step forward and two steps back" thing.

The diagnosis of "situational depression" does not apply to me. Yes, I experience deeper depression when bad stuff happens. I also experience a low-grade constant darkness even when good stuff is happening. There is a sadness in me when I experience moments of sweetness and beauty. There is a sadness in me when I am feeling genuinely happy.

It is part of me. It is an aspect of me. Owning that is as important as owning what I love about myself. It's all part of the whole that is who I am.

Even as a young child, I knew there was something different about me. The sadness I felt at *everything* ran deep.

My upbringing wasn't anything out of the ordinary: two parents, three older sisters, nice house (although haunted, for sure), dog, school, shoes, backyard, friends, bicycle.

We were never hungry or in dire financial straits, as far as I knew. We had family nearby: aunt, uncle, cousins, grandparents; no major family issues. I was raised in musical theatre and performance, debuting at the age of four on a local TV talent show with my sisters (in matching outfits, yet!) and doing my first community theatre show at the age of seven. My dad loved theatre and would pack us all into the car, take us to New York City for a long weekend, book five shows into three days, buy the Broadway score albums (and the sheet music as well), and drive us back home, singing all the way. Everything was good. Normal. And yet for me, under the surface, there was this sadness.

When I lost my dad at age twelve, I suddenly had a hook to hang the unexplained sadness on. There was finally a reason for the depression. At least, that's what made the most sense to me. Nothing really helped it, though. I saw several therapists as I grew up – my favorite being one who used to snooze through our sessions – and none really ever got to the heart of anything within me.

It took years of therapy, meds, hospitalization, natural health approaches, prayer, and lots of reading before I realized that depression is a journey. It's also a bear, a beast, a path, a tsunami, a darkness, a demon, a knight, a friend, a companion, a roommate, a critic, a protector, and – at the heart of it all – a story.

This is my story. Our story, because I know I am not alone in this experience. My hope in sharing all of this is that it helps someone to know that the darkness moves and changes and comes and goes, so you can *feel* okay with yourself even when things are not actually okay. I live with the darkness, and I haven't given up.

So please, don't give up. Not yet.

THE HUM

Enameled in fire, walking the path, the stories are shared
Stories or hearts, stories of Dads, stories of Love
Hiding something that cannot stand the light
Like sitting under the stained-glass window
storm as dark as night
The passion can be strong as ten
In my heart, this house of Life and Memory

~ rev rachel hollander, Life and Memory

Going Where I Don't Want to Go

There are stories I could share, there are feelings I could express, there are dark places I could spend long hours delving into and exploring...and I don't know that I want to go there.

And yet, to write this book, I need to go there. I need to at least visit there. To stop in and take a look. To remember. To shake up and shake loose.

For those of us who walk and live in the darkness, the visitation of places, memories, stories, feelings, ideas that might harm or scare us is not something we do willingly. This is how I skated through years of therapy when I was younger. "Why go there when it can't change?" "Why try to fix the unfixable?"

And then I learned that the only way to dispel darkness is to shine light on it. A darkened room is only scary until the light is turned on.

In the house where I grew up (my fortress), in the basement, we had two large rooms. One was a rec room that was decorated like the set from *Laugh-In.* The other room was terrifying for me. It was an unfinished space with lots of hidden corners and dark areas. It was where the furnace and hot water heater lived, as well as a large storage freezer. And it was also where the washer and dryer were...at the far end. The only light in this room was a bare lightbulb with a hanging string that hung down over the washer. We had to walk through that dark space – with all its hidden areas for monsters – and then reach out into the nothingness with open hands, find the string, and pull it to create some light.

For a young person like me, filled with imagination and more than just a touch of psychosis, the space between the door and that string was a path of terror through an endless void of vast, threatening shadows of unknowingness.

I would run – sometimes screaming – from the lighted doorway to the string. I would be shaking and sometimes crying by the time I got there. At one point I left the light on for days so that I wouldn't have to walk through that lightless space.

And that's the thing: the absence of light was the scary part. Not the darkness. Once the light was on, the darkness vanished.

That's also true for the dark places in my mind where I don't want to go.

Fun and Games

When I was a kid, one of the biggest challenges I faced was trying to find where I fit in. What crowd, what skill set, which group, all of it. I already felt strange, for no real solid reason. I already felt like I didn't "belong," with no evidence to support that. So, I found evidence.

Every summer night in my backyard the neighborhood kids would gather. They came to play in my yard because it was the biggest on the street, so, by default, I was part of the playing. Sometimes, we would play this game, which felt like absolute torture to me, called "SPUD!" The rules were overwhelming, confusing, and confounding. See if you can figure this out: a person in the middle throws a ball up into the air and yells out a number. If it's "your" number you have to run into the middle and catch the ball. Once the ball is caught, everyone must freeze. Then, the ball-catcher takes four jump-like steps toward the closest person in order to hit them with the ball, making them "it."

So, if it's *not* your number, you want to get as far away as possible. And this was where my problem with the game began. Run or wait.

If I ran, I might not get very far (I couldn't run fast). If they called my number I would have to run back, losing time as others who ran faster than me (which was everyone) got farther away, which meant it would be harder for me to hit them with the ball, because I couldn't throw either. My only other option was to wait and see if my number got called, taking the risk of it *not* being mine. If I did that, I ended up frozen by whoever caught the ball, standing there, closer than everyone – because I can't run fast – and hit effortlessly by the person throwing the ball.

And, having been hit, I would end up in the middle again, forced to throw the ball into the air and yell a number. It was confusing. It was terrorizing. I felt stuck, no matter what I chose.

Stuck. I couldn't decide what to do. I couldn't run. I couldn't catch.

And I couldn't throw the ball.

I *could* sing. I *could* cry. I *could* feel...Everything.

In my life now, I can do LOTS of things. Back then, other kids could do so many things I couldn't – things that were considered important at the time. And so I hated that game. Still, it was my backyard so I couldn't just "go home." And the sun would start setting. And the bugs would come out. And the air would get that cool dampness that sat on our skin. Then someone would yell "HIDE-AND-SEEK!" Just when I thought it couldn't get any worse.

I preferred playing "airplane crash." That was a game I could excel at. I mean, it was acting, and I was a master at acting – on stage and off. We would sit on the four-seater swing and someone would be the flight attendant (stewardess back then), someone would be the pilot (who was, of course, in love with the stewardess. Back then, that seemed to make sense, and it heightened the drama).

And then, at the right moment, we would shake the swing and enact "the crash."

We'd fling ourselves around, sometimes landing outside the swing. And then, once the crash happened, it was a test of wills to see who would wake up first. No one wanted to wake up first because if you did, that meant you weren't as hurt as the others.

The aim of this game was to be the most hurt. It was a test of wills. Kind of like the worst group therapy sessions I ended up in, where no one spoke, and the silence made you want to stand up and scream like a maniac. (Of course, you didn't, because you're in group therapy, for heaven's sake.) Inevitably, just like in group therapy, I would wake up first. No patience. Nothing was happening, and if I lay there too long a spider might walk on me. And it was boring to stay unconscious, waiting for someone else to wake up. So, I would wake up and be "the hero," helping the stewardess swim across the ocean – the span of the backyard – to the rescue boat.

Come to think of it, I didn't love that game either. At least there was no running or catching or hitting-with-the-ball involved. Honestly? I would have preferred to have been in my room, or hanging with my dad, or reading, or watching *The Carol Burnett Show*. Although I do remember loving the feel of the grass on my bare feet, the summer grass, wet and cool.

Maybe if I had been able to run faster or throw harder

and farther, liked being hidden and sought, or been the last to wake up, maybe I would have enjoyed myself more. Or maybe not.

The Machine

Starting around age ten, I had a sense of the "machine" that was running the world. It turned the planet, moved the clouds, beat my heart, kept things going.

This awareness was separate from my relationship with God, though. God was still the big man up in the clouds who I asked for things and talked to on a regular basis. The "machine" was its own entity. I would wake up on a summer morning and look out the window next to my bed. I would realize that people everywhere were awake, doing things, living lives, that my friends may have already made plans without me, that stuff was happening, and it was moving past me as I sat and watched. It wasn't totally upsetting. It wasn't all that comforting either.

The night my dad graduated from Earth School (that's how I like to think about dying) seemed like a pretty normal Wednesday night at our house. We had eaten dinner without him – it was his regular tennis night – and now I was watching TV, my sister Lisa was doing homework, and my mom was busy elsewhere in the house.

When the phone call came, I was in the bathroom. Lisa said that Mom got a call, and she had to get to the hospital; they were taking my Dad there because he had been "hurt." No other information was shared. I remember not being afraid at all, immediately checking in with my friend, God, explaining that I understood that it might take some time for my dad to recover from whatever had happened, and it was okay. I would take good care of him, as long as he was alright and came home. I was confident in God's ability to take care of my dad.

About an hour later my mom returned home. She walked past Lisa and me at the front door and went to the dining room. She turned, leaned against the wall, put her arms up into a shrug and, through tears, said, "He's gone."

I turned from her and began to walk away, audibly hearing the hum of the machine slowing down, as if someone had thrown the master switch. The hum slowed to a complete stop. It was then I realized that I had walked right into a wall and, pressed up against it, was continuing to try to move forward. It wasn't real, this wasn't happening, impossible, this had to be a dream. And still, the machine had shut down. I no longer felt alive.

Later in life, I would undergo shock treatment at a hospital in New York City. There was a moment during that treatment when I technically died. When I was defibrillated back to life, I believe the machine somehow restarted, throwing me back to the night of my dad's death. And all of the rage I couldn't express when I was twelve came out of me as I woke up. I screamed, I grabbed a nurse by the hair...I was out of control. More of that story comes later.

After that moment in our dining room, when my mother said those words and I walked into the wall, for the next twenty-four hours, nothing was real. People came into the house, brought food, sat, talked, and smoked. I sat on the couch in the front corner of the living room, and my grandpa Sid – my father's father – sat diagonally across the room from me in the big brown chair. No one spoke to either of us. Activity was all around us, and yet no one spoke directly to either of us. We looked at each other and instantly knew one another's thoughts:

disbelief, and an inability to take in what was happening.

It wasn't until the next night, at about the same time my mother had said those two words – "He's gone" – that the tears began. Suddenly, it became very real, and the fear took over. There was no way I would ever be safe in this world again.

I was totally alone and vulnerable.

I will be forever grateful to our family friends Lou and Joyce who came and found me in the upstairs alcove and literally dragged me out of the house, in my slippers, for a walk in the pouring rain around the block. They let me cry, asking no questions. It was the most generous display of love I received during that time.

Some people like to assume that the depression I was later diagnosed with began the night my dad died. This isn't true. There was evidence of it long before. What I do believe is that, with that night, I was given a hook to hang my outward symptoms on that made sense for other people. Doctors, teachers, friends, even family members could understand if I was depressed after my dad's death. And so, for many years, when asked when my depression began, I would start my story with, "When I was twelve my dad died," and there would be a nodding acceptance of that as a legitimate reason.

What I know now is that the depression was always there, from birth. The machine started when I started. That doesn't make it any easier to deal with when it makes its presence known. What it does help me to understand, though, is why, even when life is going wonderfully, even when I feel full of joy and gratitude, the depression is a part of me. Always.

The Hum

In this book I will share with you what debilitating depression can look like in my life. (Lucky you!) It isn't always debilitating. Sometimes it's just there.

How to explain the experience of living with continuous depression...Imagine that rare moment when all noise stops: TV, music, lawn mowers, washer, dryer, dishwasher, neighbors' voices. Everything is turned off, and there is no actual sound moving through the air. That's when I hear it: the hum. Not like tinnitus or an actual sound, and yet it is clearly something I hear, not imagine. It's a hum.

And it's always there, underneath all of the other sounds of our lives.

It's like a fluorescent light kind of hum. We aren't aware of it all of the time, and yet it is actually humming *all of the time.*

It doesn't impact or bother us until everything else goes quiet.

This is what my experience of living with depression is like.

I function. I swim, I chat, I drive, I do chores, I accomplish tasks. I face challenges, walk the dog, eat, watch a great show, sing, work on a jigsaw puzzle, write, read, socialize, help others, discuss, dream...I function.

All the while, the hum is there. Under it all. Never changing, never pausing.

This is the grand deception of depression – of my experience of it, anyway. I look fine. I act fine. I present myself to the world as fine. And for the most part, I guess, I am fine. It's just that I can hear the hum. All of the time.

The Goofiest Girl

For a full year after my dad died, I couldn't stop crying. I was an open wound, walking around and trying so hard to stay in my body. I was twelve, in seventh grade, and completely lost.

My family was in turmoil. Everyone was becoming seriously ill, our stability was gone, and we couldn't help each other because we were each struggling just to stand up. My mom was learning how to live alone for the first time, my sisters were each dealing with life-threatening medical issues, and in the midst of all of this, I was slowly losing my already tenuous grip on reality. And I could not stop crying.

I would wander out of classes and land in the counselor's office: Kay Brower, a Goddess among women, was the school counselor who let me sit in her office while she continued to work. She negotiated with my teachers so that I would not fail or get held back. She navigated the waters of helping me while also supporting my mom, without judgment of any kind. I wouldn't have survived without her.

The books that I carried with me 24/7 were on the topics of death, grief, and suicide. I avoided those students who would bully me, and I clung to my circle of friends who tried their best to understand what was going on with me. And I cried, continuously.

A year later, soon after eighth grade began, one of my friends said, "You have to stop crying." All I felt was the now deeply planted seed of fear that if I didn't do what she told me to do, I would be abandoned by my friends. This wasn't true, of course. It was a real fear, though. So the pendulum, having been held so far to the extreme of darkness and sadness, swung out wide and fast and locked itself at the other extreme: I became "the goofiest girl."

I began laughing all the time, being socially outlandish in my clothes and the way I talked, being funny, being lively, and making sure that everyone knew that I wasn't crying anymore. This extended into high school where I became famous for stopping an entire hallway full of students during a busy class-time-change by yelling "PENIS!" louder than all of their noise. For four years in a row, I was voted "goofiest girl" in my class. Success.

I will be forever grateful for *Annie Hall* and the fashion sense that Diane Keaton's character brought into vogue at that time. It allowed me to appear somewhat normal when, in high school, I began wearing my dad's clothes: oversized suits, pants, ties. It appeared that I was just choosing some quirky-chic way of dressing. In fact, I was wearing his clothes as an active choice. I needed him near me. If I couldn't cry, I could at least carry him around. It worked. I appeared quirky. I kept myself alive. Only my closest circle of friends knew the truth: that I was actively suicidal, that I was hurting myself, that I was hearing voices, that I was struggling to stay alive. And that I was still crying.

My persona kept me from disappearing, from being bullied, from scaring or confusing those who could never understand the pain I was feeling (although it sure did confuse and scare them in a whole other way!). It protected me. And even though the darkness of depression was still ever-present within me, my persona kept it from being seen by the world. I used it to fool therapists, teachers, family, and anyone else I encountered. I used it to help me get cast in community theatre shows or school performances. One of my most memorable of these was when I co-hosted our school's famous review show and I did my stellar imitations of

Gilda Radner's SNL characters (Baba Wawa, Roseanne Roseannadanna). I was funny. I was talented. And, behind all of that, I was totally broken.

Looking back now, I am so grateful for the goofiest girl. She kept me alive. I try not to wince or downplay her memories when high school friends bring up those famous moments of hers. I try to smile and remember to be grateful for her. She was incredibly strong. I wouldn't be here now if not for her.

Friends

I never would have survived junior high and high school without my friends.

Our circle of friends included athletes, artists, honor students, writers, popular girls, hippies...we were quite the group. All of my friends got good grades, most dated...in so many ways they were different from me. And then, in other ways, we were all so very much alike. I understood them and – this is no small deal – they understood me.

Nicole, Jody, Ina, Kathy, Amy, Tamar, Sharon, and a few others were a lifeline for me. Sometimes literally.

I didn't always tell them everything that was going on inside my head. They knew that I was the Eeyore of our group (from the Winnie-the-Pooh stories), and like those famous residents of the Hundred Acre Wood, they embraced my Eeyore-ness with total and patient acceptance.

There were darker things happening within me, though...things that I was so afraid of, I didn't want to tell anyone. I didn't want to believe they were happening. I was hearing voices. One voice, really. And it was not a very nice voice. This voice was the one that wanted me to swerve the car into a tree when I finally learned how to drive (which I had put off as long as I could). This voice was always telling me about the sharp knives in the kitchen drawer. This voice made sure that I never felt safe.

One day, I was alone at home, and the voice was especially loud. The house I grew up in was fairly big – it once housed all six of my family members. Now, I was in it alone. And there was no place to go where that voice couldn't find me.

I ran out of the house without shoes, keys, anything. I don't know where I went or how long I was gone. I just know that I ended up on Jody's front lawn, kind of dirty and fairly disoriented. Without asking a single question, Jody got me calmed down and took me back home. She knew where our hidden key was, and she got me back into the house.

I don't remember if we ever talked about this again. I just knew that I was kept safe. I was protected.

This is what my friends did for me then. It's what some of those same friends still do now.

I will always be grateful for them.

Impermanence

It took a long time for me to realize why I felt that nothing lasts. From the mundane (living spaces, employment) to the more serious (human relationships, lives of pets), I had, over the years, become keenly aware that more and more I felt a sense of nothing lasting. Eventually, I decided to explore why I felt this way.

It wasn't any big surprise that the discovery took me back to my dad.

For the first twelve years of my life, I lived with a fairly solid sense of how things worked. Yes, there had been loss and change: a dog, some guinea pigs, a friend, a grandmother. And yet, those had all somehow made sense to me. Things died, life changed. My home didn't, my world didn't. At that age and at that place in my innocence, I felt confident that I would always live in my house, my family would always be alright, and I could rely on something that felt solid.

And then, September 17, 1975, happened. The night my dad died shattered every illusion I had about consistency, about reliance, about things lasting. In that one moment, it became achingly clear that nothing would last. Ever.

Now, looking at my life – relationships, homes, pets – I can see how that realization has shaped and influenced every aspect of it.

"Enjoy the moment because nothing lasts." That's my truth. Now, to be clear, I don't say this axiom with the joy or depth of a spiritual revelation or even a T-shirt motto to live by. It's more like an omen, a foreboding, advice given by a palm reader or psychic who would warn me not to get attached to anyone, anything, or any place.

Instead of being sage advice to seize the day, it feels more like a life sentence of sadness: Don't get attached, don't love, don't feel safe, don't unpack, don't show your true self, don't let anyone in, don't want anything. Because it will all leave; it will be taken away or simply just go away.

This is not something I want to be true. This is not how I want to live. What is essential to know here is that, when I don't pay attention, this is the default where my mind and heart go. That's why I need to pay attention. Always.

Not a Real Illness

Even as a kid I remember being keenly aware of my thinking that depression wasn't a real experience, an actual condition that needed attention.

It wasn't serious, like a medical condition, even though it manifested physically.

It wasn't as dangerous as a terminal illness, even though people did die from its impact.

It didn't merit the kind of attention or sympathy that an actual sickness deserved, even though feeling unnoticed can lead to isolation and suicide.

When I was hospitalized in my twenties because of depression, I remember thinking it would be better if I had cancer or some other disease that was more real, more legitimate. I actually said this out loud: "If only I had a REAL illness – cancer, a brain tumor, something – then all of this would make sense."

I had this strong sense of guilt about the depression because, compared with people battling cancer or AIDS or something truly life-threatening, those of us living in the darkness seemed like slackers. Lazy, whining, mopey Eeyores who just didn't want to try to get better.

It also seemed like I would feel more motivated if I had a real illness. If only I had something more tangible to fight against.

When I am particularly weakened by the depression, I will experience an attack from what I call "The Knights."

One is the Red Knight from the movie *The Fisher King* (1991) with Robin Williams and Jeff Bridges. He is the haunting reminder of a traumatic moment in a character's life. He stalks, attacks, and terrifies this character. The way director Terry Gilliam showed him in the film is the perfect image for the darkness that can sometimes assault me.

The other is the Knight of the Mirrors from *Don Quixote*. Near the end of the book, Alonso Quijano's nephew-in-law-to-be attempts to shake him from his illusion of being the Knight of La Mancha. To do so, the nephew becomes the Knight of the Mirrors: he surrounds Quijano with mirrors and forces him to see himself as he is in "reality," a delusional old man full of illusions. He shatters the old Knight's dream. He breaks him, breaks his spirit, and takes away his passion for living.

When I am deep in the darkness, an attack by The Knights is devastating to my soul.

I know that depression is real, because it adds such darkness, sadness, and surrender to already deeply painful feelings. And there is no use fighting back or trying to stand up to it because there's nothing there: smoke and mirrors, only the Knights coming at me, tormenting me with their illusions of terror and destruction. Of their version of "reality". This is what it's like doing battle with my own demons. And this is why it's so hard to share this reality with those who haven't experienced the battlefield.

It Sucks

Recently, I used the phrase "pain sucks" while texting with a friend. And then I stopped for a moment to think about what that really means.

When I say that pain or depression or anxiety "sucks," I am not just complaining or disparaging these experiences. I am actually using that word more as a verb than a condemnation.

Pain, depression, and anxiety are vampires. They suck life, energy, vitality, motivation, interest, sociability, joy, fun, and gratitude from me. Or at least, they try to.

They are the shadows that creep in around 4:00 p.m. every day that tell me that I have, yet again, wasted too much time and have still not accomplished what was on my to-do list.

They are the voices that taunt me with phrases like, "You're all alone," "No one will ever want you," "Who could love someone as difficult as you?"

They are the feelings that make my stomach tight, my breath short, my heart pound, my hands shake, and my head hurt as they attempt to convince me that something is terribly wrong.

They are relentless, demonic, persistent, and determined. They have a mission I will never understand, and yet I seem to play a very important part in it; I seem to be the target.

And I guess I should clarify something here so as not to disparage vampires altogether. For years, I wanted to be a vampire. I was always fascinated by the possibility of living forever and using that quality – and the other skills that came with vampire life – for the benefit of the world. Only feeding on those who bring harm to others, using my knowledge of eternal life to heal the world from pollution, greed, and climate change, using my ethereal presence to expose corruption in politics...I had a great vision for my life as a vampire.

I would have been a good vampire.

Not at all like the ones I have lived with all of my life. The only good that has come from these vampires is that they have made me stronger, more courageous, more resilient.

I am not afraid to expose them for what they are: They are not Real. They appear to be, they want to be, and they certainly feel real. They are not "big-R" Real, though. They exist in this human experience, right alongside me, that's for sure. They do *not* have any actual power, however, in my understanding of what is Real, in a Spiritual sense.

When I am immersed in a Spiritual Practice – praying, counseling others, walking my dog, writing, singing – they have no power. When I remember who I truly am – an Individualized Expression of The Universe (or God, Spirit, whatever name works for you) – there is no fear of vampires sucking life out of me, no fear of shadows creeping or voices whispering. There is only Peace and Connection.

Here's where it gets a little tricky, though: It is an inside job. Remembering who I am, connecting with something larger than me, Knowing I am alright...all of that comes from within me.

It is not about asking for it or begging a God outside of me to "grant" it to me or wishing or hoping or bargaining. It is about Remembering. Reminding my True Self who I am.

And then, like the light of day shining on them, the vampires wither and fade and disappear – only to return if I should forget this Truth (which, of course, I do; I am still human, after all).

The Blanket and the Hum

When I was little I had, like so many did, a blankie. It was off-white with that satin quilt-like covering over it. It went everywhere with me. Yes, I was Linus from *Peanuts*. It was a cape and a picnic blanket; it was a comfort and a companion. A true security blanket.

One day, during a picnic moment, some grape juice got spilled onto it. I reluctantly turned it over to my mom to be washed and eagerly awaited its return. Except that return never happened. The blanket was thrown out. It was just gone. This was a few years before my dad was "just gone" as well.

The depression, which manifests as the low hum under everything, often feels like that blanket. It's a companion, a sense of security, something I can count on always being there.

When people talk to me about "getting rid" of the depression or ask me if I'd feel "better" if it was "cured," or even try to "heal" me "from" it, my response is always the same: Who would I be without it? How would I feel without it? How would I know that I'm safe?

This hum has always been a part of who I am, at least in this incarnation. I've heard it all of my life. I didn't understand what it was back when I was younger and first encountered it. I remember thinking that it was a house noise or a radio left on somewhere. It didn't register that it was inside of me, in my head.

Until the night my dad died.

I remember distinctly, immediately after my mom said the words "He's gone," hearing the sound of a large machine whirring down, as if someone shut off the main switch. The mechanism in my head that kept the hum going suddenly had the plug kicked out from it, and there was this slowly diminishing mechanical sound.

Maybe the "hum machine" had overloaded with that information and needed to shut down to reboot. It did reboot; within twenty-four hours the hum returned.

Today, after a few months of actually feeling...well, "normal" (read as: good, happy, functional, not sad), I noticed that the hum was louder. I had noticed some of my behaviors in the past few days that would have been clues to the hum's return had I actually been paying attention: not getting out of bed right away, napping, eating unconsciously, withdrawing, procrastinating. I didn't acknowledge these road signs, so naturally the hum was going to get louder so that I would take note.

The main difference in looking at this moment compared with moments like it in the past is a large one: no judgment.

I don't feel like a failure or that I am a bad person or that I've done something wrong or that I need "fixing." It's just the hum. And it's just a little louder. So, pay attention. What do I need to do? Any or all of these:

Get to bed earlier.

Make healthier, wiser, more conscious eating choices.

Go to the pool.

Walk my dog Maddie one extra block (if I can).

Read my homework.

Write.

Tell someone (someone who won't judge, condemn, or try to fix me).

Gently, do what needs done.

Listen for The Universe (God/Spirit) and move when told.

Most importantly, I need to choose to do what will feel productive. And not judge what I am not able to do.

When I was little and feeling afraid or overwhelmed, sometimes that blanket helped me feel safe and comforted, reminding me that I was okay where I was, just as I was. It was a placeholder for me, for my sense of belonging and refuge. It protected me from...everything.

When it was taken from me – just gone – I felt exposed to the world, unsheltered from whatever might come at me.

Which is also how I felt when my dad was just gone. Which is the same deep feeling that bubbles up when anyone talks about getting rid of the hum.

I don't need the blanket. I don't need the depression.

I need to feel safe. I need to feel protected. I need to feel like myself.

Somehow, in some way that I cannot quite define, the hum does that for me.

10 WEST

In a world that's filled with darkness
We all reach for the light
Driven by desperation
Making mistakes to be right
We know better and we still get lost
And though they do the same, we pay the cost
Of freedom, of light, of life….
What happens after, nothing fades, nothing dies
You're still left searching on your own
For purpose, for fight
For your life

~ rev rachel hollander, 10 West

The Waiting Room of My Emotions

As a young woman, I was tormented for years by darkness, by a voice telling me it was inhabiting my body. To say that I was unsteady would be an understatement.

By the time I was twenty-three, that voice had finally moved on. I was elated. I thought I was ready to move forward, to create a new life for myself. And I made quite possibly the most unwise decision of my life. I decided to move from my hometown in northeast Ohio to New York City.

Picture it: an emotionally unbalanced woman living with depression, still somewhat psychotic, moving from the Midwest to NYC. Brilliant, right?

It didn't take long in that city for the depression to take a quantum jump. Manhattan is not an easy place for a sensitive soul, and I walked the city feeling vulnerable and so fragile. I managed, barely, to keep it together for about a year and a half.

Eventually, however, I wasn't able to keep a job, and, as I began to slip into an ever-deepening darkness, I refused to leave my apartment. I was afraid of everything. My body began to break down: my physical health became a reflection of my internal experience and manifested as illness.

My doctor, playing catch-up with all of the symptoms and ailments that were appearing, kept prescribing medications to "fix" me. Given that opportunity, I began to collect meds.

One night in November 1987, in the depths of sadness and desperation, I sat on the bed and started color-coding all of the pills I had. I then organized them into piles in order of which was easiest to swallow.

As proof that the Universe has always had my back, at just the moment when I was ready to begin the process of taking those pills, a very dear friend called me and started the conversation with this: "Whatever you are doing, stop. Just stop."

Within a few days I was admitted to an unlocked psych unit at a hospital in the city.

By a few days into my stay, I had become the model patient. I believed that no one could really help me and that nothing I could say would change anything, so I used my skills as an actor to show everyone what a great patient I could be. And honestly, I thought the hospital was WONDERFUL! I got three meals a day (including pudding, a definite plus), didn't have to do my own laundry, didn't need a job, and got to play bingo on a regular basis (I was queen of bingo!). We had art therapy several times a week, and I loved the art room. I became quite skilled at improvised rug-hook projects and painting really gloomy artwork.

I also helped everyone: I supported the staff, I counseled other patients, and I was an ambassador to other patients' visitors. And most importantly, I made my own visitors as comfortable as possible. I mean, it was hard for them to see me there, so I made it easier by being "fine." I kept everything at a distance, including my own pain and sadness.

I became the Analogy Queen, able to articulate my experience beautifully using images and examples, song lyrics or movie scenes, without ever actually expressing what I was really feeling.

One of my best analogies was the "waiting room of my emotions." When I was feeling nothing or couldn't find words to express the feelings, I would describe the worst medical waiting room you could imagine: green dingy walls, flat vinyl benches with cracks in them (the kind that pinch your legs), really old magazines. I would explain that I was left to sit in this room while all my feelings and emotions were having a meeting on the other side of the door. Every so often, one would peek out through the door and condescendingly say, "We'll be with you in a moment, when we're ready." I would continue to sit, feeling nothing, separated. When asked by the staff at the hospital what was going on, I would explain, "They're not quite ready for me yet."

There was a safety in this. Uncomfortable, yes. A little awkward, definitely. Safe, though.

After several weeks, I was given a day pass to go see *Les Misérables* with my sister Anita, who lived in NYC. I was doing so well, as far as the doctors were concerned, that this was anticipated to be my last pass before I would be released.

I had successfully convinced everyone on the unit, with the exception of one or two nurses, that I was cured, that it had been a minor bout of depression typical of a young woman in her early twenties, and that I could go back out into the world, medicated and functional.

About six weeks into my stay, the process of release was begun. I felt strangely satisfied, as if my game of fooling them was some kind of success. I was also scared, though. I knew I wasn't any better – just a more talented actor than I thought.

Clare's Story

There was a woman on the psych unit who I'll call Clare. We were both twenty-four – the two youngest patients on the unit. She totally fascinated me. She didn't speak. And being the person I am, the kind who never STOPS speaking, I was immediately drawn to her. I thought, how wonderful it must be to never speak. I really admired this quality and wondered what it must be like to carry that much power: the simple and impressive power of silence.

Naturally, I spent as much time talking to her as possible. I talked to her all day long: "Hey, Clare, how's your day going?" "Nice nightgown, Clare." "Clare, do you like pudding, too?" It was a constant one-sided dialogue. She never replied or even acknowledged that she heard me.

One night, I was watching a movie in the common room, and Clare was sitting behind me. The commercial break was running really long. Suddenly, I heard Clare's voice from behind me say, "That's an awful lot of commercials." She SPOKE! I was so excited! I didn't want to show it, though, afraid it might scare her off. I turned my head slightly to the side and replied, "Why, yes! Yes that IS a lot of commercials!" I was so thrilled to have shared this moment with her! I felt like she had granted me a tiny invitation into her world.

Just a day or two later, on December 15, 1987, I saw that Clare was on the phone. This was odd because she never used the phone. We were all told not to let her take calls on the public phone we shared, though we weren't told why. And yet, there she was, at the nurse's station, using their phone, so I assumed it was alright.

I watched her for a few moments, trying to gauge the essence of the call and how she was handling it. Then the call ended, and she went to her room. A few moments later, still in her nightgown, she walked right past me as I sat in the hallway. I said, "Hey, Clare." She continued to walk, calmly and silently, past all of us. She walked out of the unit, got into the elevator, went to the roof, and jumped. She landed on the FDR East River Highway.

I am not sure how long it was before the whole unit was called into the multipurpose room. Somehow, the doctor managed to tell us what Clare had done without totally losing control of every patient there. We were told that her name had not been released to the media, so we should line up at the nurse's station to make calls to our family or loved ones to let them know not to worry when they saw the news.

I felt stunned. I felt jealous of her courage. I felt ashamed of my own cowardice. I felt so many things – everything and nothing, all at once. I calmly got in the line to call my sister; I didn't want her to go through that moment of seeing the news and thinking she had lost me.

One woman asked if she could cut in line in front of me because she needed to call her husband, letting me know that his worrying about her was somehow more important than my sister's concern for me. A husband rated much higher than just a sister. The internal scream that had begun with the news of Clare's action was now getting louder and, at any moment, was going to be outside of me and heard by everyone.

My favorite nurse was on duty that night and I asked her, privately, if I could have some time alone in the quiet room. I explained that I had been acting this whole time, that all of the pain, rage, sorrow, all of it was ready to blow, and I just wanted to be in a safe space when it first came out. After a few minutes in that room, I would be ready to talk and I would finally begin, for real, the work I was there to do. She agreed.

It was like something broke loose in me, and everything I had never said or shared was ready to come out. The nursing staff – a most amazing group of women, and one man – was so encouraging and ready to support me in whatever way I needed.

The doctor, on the other hand, did not see the situation in the same way. He saw this as an uncontrollable outburst that, naturally, needed to be controlled.

What he had completely missed – the entire time I had been there – was that I had been *too* controlled up until that moment. I had been totally controlling every aspect of myself: my emotions, what I told the staff, how I shared myself. There was never a moment when I was not keeping things well contained. This moment, however, through Clare's final act of independence and courage, was my moment to let EVERYthing out. At last.

Years of containment and control were ready to burst forth and be seen, heard, and healed.

Sadly, the doctor missed this completely. This loss of control, in his eyes, was not to be allowed. He labeled me "a danger" and offered only one solution: to medicate me. Heavily. He doubled the doses of all of the meds I had been taking.

Within hours I was unable to walk without the support of the wall. I could barely stay awake, and my ever-present hand tremors had become so debilitating that writing in my journal was nearly impossible.

I realized that there was nothing I could do anymore. It felt as if the people who were there to help me didn't want to hear what I had to say, so I chose to stop speaking. What I had admired in Clare was now to become the way I wanted to stay. I hated the doctor for his egotistical inadequacies, and I was going to choose. Choose to give him nothing. I was choosing to simply give up. I didn't care what happened to me after that. The only thing left that I had control over was my own self, my own life.

In my desperation, I attempted the only act I was capable of: to harm myself. I wasn't as courageous as Clare. I chose the peanut butter cookie route.

Allow me to explain.

This was before the friendly SSRI days of Prozac. I was taking Lithium and an MAO inhibitor, as well as some other antiquated antidepressants, all of which caused some powerful side effects. The MAO inhibitor had some serious dietary restrictions. If the naughty foods were eaten, it could potentially cause a brain hemorrhage. One of those forbidden foods was peanut butter.

Picture this: A nurse enters a small kitchen area to find me with my sweater pockets, hands, and mouth jammed full of peanut butter cookies. It was, as far as I know, the first and only reported case of suicide attempt by peanut butter cookies. Sadly, they were artificially flavored. It wasn't even real peanut butter. Hey, in that environment, it was the best I could do.

Looking back, I'm able to laugh – heartily. I mean, imagine the lawsuit, the headlines, the eulogy!

The doctors did not find this funny at all. As far as they

were concerned, this stunt I pulled with the cookies was a viable suicide attempt, and for that act, I lost my freedom.

My street clothes were taken from me, I had to wear hospital pajamas only, my movement was limited to the unit, and I was assigned a one-on-one nurse who was with me every moment.

I was not permitted to close the bathroom door, ever. I was monitored in the shower. I had no privacy with visitors and was watched as I slept. Game over.

Friends would come and go, or – because it was so painful for them – they would sometimes not come at all. It didn't matter anymore. In my darkness, I knew that no one could understand.

Shocked

On December 31, the psychiatric resident sat me down and explained that the team had run out of options with me. The meds were only causing me to be more doped-up, out of it, and uncommunicative. It was clear that I was no longer the cooperative patient I had been, and there was only one choice left: ECT, electroconvulsive therapy.

Shock treatment. The only question I asked was if it could potentially kill me. He said that there were some risks. I told him to sign me up.

I had been ready to yield to the emotional tsunami that had been building within me my entire life. I was finally ready to let the truth out, every last ugly bit of it. And I was denied that opportunity.

So, instead, feeling as if I had been given no other option, I chose to surrender to the medical establishment, who chose to silence me, in the hopes that they would end my life for me.

My logic at that moment was simple: something goes wrong, malpractice suit, my mom gets a lot of money, I am out of pain and no longer a burden. Everyone wins.

Being twenty-four, I was allowed to sign all of the release forms myself. This would become a major issue for my family as they questioned the hospital's logic of allowing a suicidal and depressed in-patient to sign her own papers for anything. But the hospital's perspective was that, because I had voluntarily signed myself into the unit, I was now permitted to make all healthcare decisions myself.

The night before the first treatment, I sat on my bed and thought, "How did I get here? How did this happen?" I reflected on my entire life, every joyful moment and every disappointment. Every celebration and every tragedy. And as I did this, I realized that - in the state of mind that I was in - the darkness overcame the light in every example. The sadness had won out.

Somehow, I had gotten from there, from that whole past world, to here, a psych unit, about to have electricity used on my brain. Hoping, in some way, that it would kill me so that I would be off the hook for living the rest of my life.

On January 1, 1988, the first treatment was given. What was most interesting about the preparation for this moment was what happened the day before. My favorite nurse, knowing that I was a creature of habit and very aware that being thrown off from my sense of what was "normal" could potentially increase a feeling of anxiety, advised me to make a list of everything I did each day, all of my routines. Did I brush my teeth first in the morning or wash my face? Did I soap up in the shower before or after I washed my hair? Which were my most comfortable items of clothing? Did I pray at night? What were my favorite foods? I was told that I would remember nothing about my everyday life. And, if the ECT worked, I wouldn't remember I had been sad. The reasons would no longer matter; the feelings would just disappear, and there would be no need to find out what caused them anymore.

The treatments began and went as scheduled, every other day, early in the morning. And, sure enough, every time I woke up after a treatment, everything about my life was brand new. On those days, I would be happily surprised by the new and cool clothes I was given to wear, thankful to whoever left them for me and happy that they were so comfortable. Lunch and dinner were a treat; I would wonder who knew me so well that they ordered pudding for me. I loved pudding! Visitors would come and go, apparently having some very important conversations with me that I could not remember. Sadly, those conversations never came back to me.

I was expected to go through seven to ten treatments and then be reevaluated. The one thing the staff noticed about my sessions was that my brain would seize longer than the normal or expected time (approximately fifteen seconds). There was some suspicion around this. Not enough to stop doing it, though. Until the seventh treatment.

The following series of events was shared with me several times after the incident took place. I have no memory of any of it happening or how many times the details had to be repeated to me before they became something I remembered on my own.

During the seventh session, my brain would not stop seizing. There was concern and then a decision to inject my IV with Valium to force the seizure to stop. It worked — really well. Apparently, I died.

I was then rushed somewhere and defibrillated to be brought back to life. When I came back, I awoke screaming, grabbed a nurse by the hair, and began thrashing her head around. Immediately, more Valium was injected into me to get me under control again, and I was knocked out. My theory is that wherever I was, I was probably chatting with my dad and didn't want to leave. Their choice to yank me back into life made me furious. Looking back from the vantage point of hindsight, it makes more sense for me to believe that my Dad would not let me stay with him, as he knew I had more work to do here on the planet, and he helped to send me back. Regardless, I wasn't happy about any of it.

Needless to say, the shock treatment came to an end that

day. They decided that it wasn't really working for me. And the new theory was that I wasn't dealing with depression after all; what I actually had was a seizure disorder that could be treated easily with new medications.

Although I wasn't thrilled about the idea of any new medication, I was so very happy to receive the new diagnosis. "Seizure disorder" carried much more credibility than depression did. It was more tangible. It seemed to have more validity. At that time, the common view of depression – in my estimation, anyway – was that it was the person's own fault and not a real disease, and the general response was to tell the person suffering to get off their pity pot and start living. With a seizure disorder, I couldn't be blamed anymore; it wasn't my fault. This was great news!

So, all of the depression and anxiety meds went away and were replaced by new, stronger medications. And there was hope now. The diagnosis of seizure disorder seemed to make everyone on the team happy as well. I was given another month or so to "heal up," given my new prescriptions and my new diagnosis, and sent out the door of the hospital, back into New York City. No longer a depressed person, I was now a hopeful young woman with a seizure disorder, ready to take on the world!

The Return

About a month after the shock treatment debacle, I was still dazed and heavily medicated for the supposed seizure disorder. My mom wanted to make everything better, so she took me to one of my favorite places: Disney World.

The photos from this adventure are creepy, to say the least. I have dead eyes, doll's eyes, shark eyes. There's no life behind them. And my smile is the smile of someone slightly overwhelmed and maybe a bit confused as to exactly where she is.

My mom had the best intentions in mind. She knew I loved it there, and her hope was that Disney World would remind me of feeling happy. I'll give you one guess how that turned out.

Within a month after returning to NYC, I was back in the hospital. It hadn't taken long to discover that there was no seizure disorder. This was devastating news. Whatever was wrong with me was once again my fault. The medical reasons for it went away. This caused me to spiral even deeper and into a much darker space, one of total submission. There was no more fight left in me. It had won, and I was ready to let go of my life.

The discussion at the hospital centered on what could be done with me. It was clear that I couldn't function in the all-too-real world of Manhattan, so the hospital staff gave me the ultimate ultimatum: agree to being admitted to the locked unit at Bellevue with the "incurably insane" people—or leave New York City. I was basically kicked out of NYC. At the time, it was baffling to me. Looking back, it's actually a badge of honor that I proudly own!

They began the process of discharging me into someone else's care – namely my mother's – who might then be forced into the process placing me into a group home where I could be monitored for the rest of my days. Bingo and pudding. It sounded lovely.

Upon my release from the hospital a few weeks later, the psychiatrist who had treated me informed my mother that what she was getting back was her twenty-five-year-old daughter:

who would never develop organizational thinking;
who would never be able to hold a job;
who would never live independently;
who would need to live in a group home;
who would always need to be medicated.

His words of wisdom? "Good luck."

The In-Between

When I left New York City, I retreated to Hudson, New York, a small town a short train ride away from the city. I lived with friends, my sister Celia taught me to drive stick-shift, I was able to handle a part-time job serving popcorn at the local movie theatre, and I traveled back and forth to the city to meet with my psychiatrist.

This was also when I met Dr. Michael Shaffer — a chiropractor and so much more. He healed me and guided me and taught me. The biggest lesson I learned from Dr. Michael was that, when I was ready to be healed, Healers would show up. I just had to be ready. After a couple of months living in Hudson, it was time for me to return to Ohio. There was no way I would ever live in NYC again, and the people who had been kind enough to take me in were pretty much ready for me to move on!

I moved back to Cleveland and into the home of my mom and stepdad.

It wasn't my home – the home of my childhood. These weren't my "parents" as a unit. And I wasn't a child. However, I was still fairly broken.

At this time, I was in a letter-writing relationship with my beloved friend Michael Devon in NYC. He encouraged me to take things one small goal at a time, to not leap into a self-defeating spiral before taking a first step. His letters encouraged me and made me laugh. When I shared my anxieties with him, his response was, as always, part yelling at me and part loving me. He pointed out how I always saw the endgame without realizing all the possibilities that could happen along the way. And, because of this, I overwhelmed myself.

Michael teased that if I returned to school, I would meet and fall in love with my first professor, and we would run off together to start a farm and grow potatoes, and I would find lasting happiness. Or on my first day at a waitressing job, a millionaire would be swept away by my charm and take me away to live on a yacht. Michael was hilarious and very kind. He was trying to teach me to BE IN the moment I was in, instead of trying so desperately to just suffer through it. He was showing me how to find the hidden gifts in being right where I was.

Michael, in his unique way, was teaching me how to get from there to here. How to keep going forward, to not get stuck.

It took me years to understand that. And Michael left the planet before I was able to show him how his advice became a lasting gift to me.

Overwhelmed

Not long after my return to Ohio, I actually tried to get a job waiting tables at a small diner that I loved. It looked like work that I could navigate: a handful of tables and a counter, lots of regulars, nice owners.

They gave me the menu to study and asked me to return in a few days for a "quiz." My brain could barely retain a single phone number or directions to places I had been many times before. When I returned for the quiz, I just broke down crying.

I felt like a failure. I felt like a mentally ill person. I felt like I belonged in a hospital or group home. I felt nothing like my own self.

I had a dream to become a cantor, like my dad. To sing in temple and be the "voice of Israel, the voice of God." I investigated the process: I would need to return to college, get a BA, then go to Israel to study, then more study at a theological university, and then, and then, and then...I was immediately overwhelmed. How would I ever be able to do ANY of that?

I felt as if I was a fragile, incapable person. That I was what the doctors said that I would be.

And yet, as always, there was an Essence within me (call it God, Spirit, Mystery, whatever word works) that kept assuring me that I was not what they described. That my living in the darkness was going to be my gift, my way of navigating the world. It was going to be the best tool I have in my toolbox.

This was a tricky notion to believe.

The Impossible

Eventually, I convinced my mom that it was a safe bet for me to get an apartment with a friend of a friend. That, by living with her, I would have our mutual friend, Carl, nearby and everything would be alright. And it was, for a while.

I was hired by a gas station near my mom's house, and I worked the night shift (10:30p-7:30a) which provided me with quiet, with stories of interesting characters, and with the opportunity – at 3:00a – to hit all of the speaker buttons on the pumps and sing show tunes out into the night. The local police officers and I became good friends.

The desire to do something a little creative returned to my consciousness, and working nights made that challenging. So, I left that job and was able to discover new skills by working at an animal hospital. The duties included front desk/reception work as well as assistant/technician work. I really enjoyed it! I spent all day with dogs and cats, and some people as well. And I had my evenings free again.

One of the most tender memories I have of working at the animal hospital – a moment that now, in retrospect, shows me how the path to becoming a minister was clear – was when one of our older clients came with his aging beagle. These two guys had been together through a lot. And, sadly, the beagle was suffering. His owner chose to put his buddy to sleep before things got too difficult for him. And he asked me if I would sit with him during this.

He had me hold his dog so that he could be face-to-face with him. We sat together for a few minutes before the doctor came into the room. The man cried and held my hand while petting his dog's head. He shared stories of their adventures.

As the dog's soul left his body, this kind gentleman sat, holding his buddy's head, and said a tender good-bye.

I walked him to the door and he hugged me.

The best part of this story? Three weeks later, he returned with his new beagle puppy!

Working at the animal hospital provided me with countless opportunities to show and share love with people, to forgive those who -- I felt -- did not treat their pets well, and, to forgive myself for holding judgment against those people.

During this time I was also gifted my first cat, Lestat, who was rescued at two weeks. I cared for him and became his "momma cat," and we began twelve years of adventures together.

It was also during this time that I returned to theatre.

One of the "glitchy" after-effects from the ECT was that my memory (long and short term) never fully returned. I was concerned about learning lines and remembering blocking and being able to find my way around a stage like I had before.

Once again, something larger than me had my back.

Over the next few years I had the opportunity to play Agnes in *Agnes of God*, Eva Peron in *Evita*, Mary Magdalene in *Jesus Christ Superstar*, and roles in several other productions, all directed by skilled professionals who pushed me to do and be more than I ever thought possible.

Soon, I was not only living on my own and working but

also socializing, performing, singing, laughing, and living a life that I was told would be impossible for me.

Continuing in therapy and still taking meds, I began to look more deeply into my own abilities, the abilities that were given to me and that were being fostered by that Essence that I called God.

There was more to come for me. I was being led, like Jacob, on a journey. I just had to keep trusting.

30th Birthday

When I was thirteen, I made a deal with myself that if things didn't get better by the time I was thirty, I had permission to take myself out. I figured – in my thirteen-year-old brain – that thirty was a fair enough age to have created a good life. I reasoned that one had to be a complete failure to have not gotten it together by the time they were thirty.

Having set that as my goal, I squeaked through high school, barely graduating, and made it about halfway through a semester at college. I mean, it didn't really matter, right? I wasn't really going to be here to worry about not being successful. I just had to make it to my thirtieth birthday.

When I was twenty-eight, heading toward twenty-nine, things were not looking good. I had failed at any relationship I attempted. I was working a job I hated. And a week before my twenty-ninth birthday, my one "wait-for-them-because-someday-they'll-figure-it-out" true love called to tell me that they were getting married. All was pretty much lost. Any work I had done on myself to become "happy" hadn't worked, and I was facing what potentially looked to be my last year on the planet.
On a whim, encouraged by my mom, I decided to take a huge leap and put myself "out there." I prepared my résumé, dug out my (by then) six-year-old head shot, and sent them to a local theatre company I had volunteered with back in junior high school. They were hiring, and I was thinking good thoughts. I heard nothing.

Three months later I was fired from the job I hated and became unemployed. I was moving to an even smaller apartment and was feeling lost...again. Having heard nothing from the theatre company, I figured that this was just another sign letting me know that my thirtieth birthday deal was a good plan.

My mom, being the woman she is, encouraged (well, nagged) me to call and follow up with the company to see what was up. I was reluctant to do that. If they didn't want me, why should I bother? So I did nothing.

Within forty-eight hours, a message showed up on my answering machine: an offer to audition for the company.

My audition piece was a story taken from a letter written by a friend who was in jail. The story resonated with me deeply, so it was easier to memorize and much more convincing than any traditional monologue could have been. And it worked.

I joined the company seven months before my thirtieth birthday.

Because the deal I had made with myself – that I would end my life on the New Year's Eve of my thirtieth year if my life hadn't turned around in some way or if I had not found a way to be happy – it was essential that some serious thought was going to need to take place that day. So, on my thirtieth birthday, I held a summit. In meditation, I envisioned a boardroom, high in the sky, with floor-to-ceiling windows and lots of bright light streaming in. There was a long boardroom table in the room. At one end sat my dad and God, who appeared as an old man, clean-cut and looking great in his suit. At the other end, all the way across the room, I sat alone.

God: Alright, Rachel. You know why we're here.
 Dad is silent—yet smiling at me.
Me (clearing my throat): Yes.
God: Are you going to stay or go?
 Dad is looking at me, his eyes shining.
Me: Well, I would like to know if there is any room for discussion. For negotiation.
 God and *Dad* look at one another, nod, look back at me.
Dad: What would you like to talk about?
Me: Well, it seems that this is not the easiest decision for me to make. I mean, life here on earth is challenging and sometimes just plain hard.
 Nods shared.
Me: So, what happens if I feel really sad? Or frustrated? What happens when nothing is going right and I feel all alone? What about really bad days? What about the dark nights of the soul?
God: Those will happen.
Dad: We don't expect you to be happy all the time, Rachel.
Me (pausing):   Okay...What *do* you expect then?
God: Either you are staying, or you are not staying. That

decision needs to be made today.

Dad: The only parameter to this agreement, Rachel, is that suicide is off the table. It will no longer be considered a viable option.

Me: No matter what?

God and *Dad:* No matter what.

God: You will feel anything and everything you want – or don't want – to feel. Moments of depression will return, and you will feel all of it.

Dad: You will also feel all of the happiness of life as well. There will be no limits on the feeling of anything.

God: However – and let me make this very clear – if you choose to stay, suicide is completely off the table. Simply put, not acceptable. No negotiation.

Dad: And, at some point, you will learn that Gratitude is the key to getting you through even the darkest of times. Gratitude will always carry you from the past to the now, from there to here. Trust me on this one. Remember how I lived.

I agreed to stay.

DEPRESSION, A PRIMER

Where does the time go during each day?
Where do I go when I lose my self?
Walking a little too close to the edge of this abyss
Closer than is safe for me.

~ rev rachel hollander, Deeper In

"A blow, expected, repeated, falling upon a bruise with no
smart or shock of surprise, only a dull and sickening pain and
the doubt whether
another like it could be borne."

- Evelyn Waugh, *Brideshead Revisited*

It Feels Like....

To me, depression at its worst feels like crushing. A crushing of the spirit. Such aloneness that even the Gratitude of knowing there are people out there doesn't make a difference. (And I really want to be someone for whom Gratitude ALWAYS makes a difference.)

There is a sense of being a complete burden even to those who say, directly, that you are not. Their words don't change the feeling that they are carrying you along, dragging you along, patiently – for now – until their patience wears thin.

It's not a question of "get over it". For those who love you would never say that. Those who understand would never say those kinds of phrases; they know better. Those phrases bury someone like me. Get over what? My life? Every failure? Every loss? Every time someone left, voluntarily or otherwise? Every time I tried to accomplish something, got excited about something, had a passion for something, and then had that thing – whatever it is – crash and burn? Or leave, or disappear? Trying and failing, that is the pattern. Changing and relapsing. It would be easier if I were doing heroin; at least there are real treatments for physical addictions. When it is a depression relapse, there isn't anything for that. Except a return to therapy. And even THAT feels like a failure.

These days, it is a darkness that understands itself: an awake darkness. When I was younger, that wasn't the case; the darkness was one of no awareness. I felt like depression was happening *to* me, and I had no control over it. Now, I understand it more. That doesn't make the dark days easier. If anything, it makes them worse. They can be filled with guilt along with the fear.

On those days, I walk around like a shell. There is a deadness inside of me that is frightening.

I might believe I'm having a heart attack, until I can convince myself I'm not.

I might cry for hours – the kind of crying that comes from the deepest place inside. I cry like a hurt child, a lonely one, a left-behind one who doesn't want to reach out because...well... who would understand?

It feels at once empty, painful, and numb, like being under anesthesia or coming out from under it.

It feels guilt-ridden, purposeless, hopeless, and humiliating.

It's frustrating and familiar. It's sometimes safe and quiet, and yet uncomfortable.

It feels like being lost in a foreign country.

It's wasteful. Stupid. Ungrateful. Lonely. Recurring, like a stalker.

It never stops.

It never says, "Oh, I'll take a day off so you can feel something different, so you can get back up, find your feet." No. It never says that.

Depression doesn't give out breaks. It doesn't give a day off or time off.

Sometimes it feels like an assault.

It comes barreling down, like the Red Knight.

It stands strong like the Knight of the Mirrors.

It just blasts...and hits...

And then, it hums...it returns to being the underlying hum.

That humming time is the closest it comes to feeling like a breather.

Still...it's humming under everything...all of the time.

It never stops...

It never lets go...

It never lets me go...

It's a Pain

Depression is a pain. Physically, emotionally, mentally, socially, spiritually, practically...In every possible way.

It saps energy. It steals joy. It dampens motivation. It disrupts peace.

It elevates, enhances, and expands anything that might be considered a "little" problem. Anything that most people would think was nothing – that could be handled easily and moved through without effort – depression can take a molehill and make a most impressive mountain out of it.

It is relentless. Intrusive. Pushy. Oppressive. Mean-spirited. Lethargic. And, like God, it plays no favorites, lets no one off the hook.

All day long, great ideas will come to me, ways I can make the day better: work out, spend time with a jigsaw puzzle, clean, write, play piano, apply for employment... so many things I could be doing. And yet, so many hours pass and I realize that I haven't moved. Imagine: an hour, two hours will go by and I haven't moved. Not crying, not feeling sad, not anxious, not really feeling anything.

Just sitting.

Even more fascinating are the things that I choose not to do. Sometimes skipping a medication or supplement I've been taking daily. I know it's helping me. I know my body needs the support. I will simply look the other way. No reason. No malice. No energy put forth about it whatsoever. Just...nothing.

Sometimes it's like that, just nothing. Sometimes depression is a pain. Sometimes it's the absence of pain. Sometimes it's the memory of a pain. Like the dull ache of a bruise or a broken bone trying to heal, trying simply to mend.

Sometimes it is the absence of everything. Which, in a strange way, is a relief from the pain. And, at the same time, feeling nothing can be deeply disturbing.

If I had a choice, I guess I'd take the pain.

The Knot

Depression is kind of like a knot. Not one tied with really thick rope, more like the kind tied with some fine thread or a silver necklace chain. The kind that, as you attempt to untie it, you end up tightening another part of it. A multi-knotted knot. You loosen a piece, and another one tangles. Or you get through a couple and then discover that it's actually still tied, just in a different place.

It slips in my hand. I have to balance my wrists on my

knees and try not to lose the progress I've made. Because that's the worst part. Progress is made, the knot gets clearer, and then there's slippage. And it retightens.

As much as others would like to help -- and offer to help -- the knot is of my own making. It requires my full focus. Only my hands can untie it. Getting help only makes it more challenging the next time the knot happens.

There is always a next time.

Even in the midst of the most "normal" or "high functioning" days, it's there. The knot. Tying, loosening, re-tangling.

On the completely opposite end of that knot metaphor, however, is God (Spirit, whatever name works for you). The idea of God being a safety line for me, always there, always holding steady, always ready for me to grab onto to pull me through. This image – as far from the knot as possible – reminds me of a beautiful poem by William Stafford called *The Way it Is,* in which he describes life (and faith and anything that keeps us anchored) as a thread. That, as everything else changes, the thread does not change.

It is too difficult for others to see the thread, or to understand our explanation of it.

The thing is, it is essential that we never let go of the thread. Even though we can't control everything that is unfolding around us, even while others seem flummoxed by our grip on it, we must hold on to the thread.

This thread never becomes knotted, is never tangled. It is always there for us.

We can never let go of it.

The Afternoon

The tendrils start to creep up usually around 3:40 p.m. There's no reason for it, nothing that causes it, no precipitating factors. They just start to wrap around and take hold.

It's the strangest sensation...maybe like having a roommate who I don't see often and yet they are still there, sometimes being cool and easygoing and sometimes totally messing with my personal space.

Or like the morning after the death of someone close. I wake up and, for just a brief moment, I can believe that the death was just a dream and couldn't possibly be true. And then, slowly, it begins: like water rising above my feet during a flood...no, it's heavier, like tar being poured over my head, thick and viscous and heavy, slowly encompassing me, pulling me down with its gravity.

There's suddenly the tightness in the throat. Next comes the stomach, the solar plexus. Gripping, contracting, trembling. Hard to take a deep breath. Slightly nauseous. It could be "just" some anxiety or worry. It isn't though...it is scary. It is painful. The feeling that tears are ready to come. Deep breaths can't hold them back. They push their way up and out.

Why, though? What's the cause?

Is it because I dare to question its hold on me? Because I let myself believe that the darkness might be lifting, receding? Because I try to allow hope and possibility to become stronger than the darkness?

Oh, darkness, my friend, nothing could ever really be stronger than you. We both know that. There's no need to prove your strength to me.

Choices, Choices, Choices....

Here's the thing.

Depression will try to trick us into thinking a lot of things that are simply not true. Here are some of the big lies it throws at us:

1. That we don't have choices.

2. That we are always going to be the way we are now.

3. That we are always going to feel the way we feel now.

4. That we are unworthy of...(fill in the blank: love, friendship, happiness, etc.)

So, let me break this down right here and now.

One: We have choices. All human beings have choices, all the time. Sometimes the options suck, sometimes they all seem delicious.

We have the choice to get up and put on pants or to stay

in bed and hide.

We have the choice to drink a glass of water (because we know we will feel better) or to skip it. We have the choice to socialize or cocoon. We have all of the choices.

We also, like every other human being, have to accept the consequences of those choices.

Staying in bed might mean losing our employment. Not drinking water might cause us to become dehydrated and feel crappy. The extreme of socializing (or cocooning) might exhaust or isolate us.

Two: Nothing is ever the way it was. Even in the last five minutes things have changed. If everything was the way it was before, we would be cavemen and there would be no internet. Don't buy it. Everything changes, nothing stays the same. The bad, the good, all of it. This too shall pass.

Three: See Number Two. Yes, it feels very real. I understand. I feel that way sometimes. And then I remember that it is a lie. THIS TOO SHALL PASS! All of it! When we feel good, it will pass. When we feel terrible, it will pass. The throughline for all of this is, yes, you

guessed it, Gratitude. And Patience. We have had
moments of feeling alright. They will return. Hold on. Do
not give up.

Four: Yeah, so for this one, depression is just being an
obnoxious bully. Every single being on this planet – from
plant, to insect, to mammal, to human – is worthy of
existing. (Okay, yes, I am still working out the spider
thing...sometimes things take time!) Michael taught me in
one his best songs that we don't have to prove ourselves
to be worthy. We don't have to do or be anything other
than the amazing creation that we are in order to be
worthy.

Is this easy to remember? No. Does it sometimes feel
true? Yes. Is it true? NEVER.

We are each essential pieces in the Cosmic Jigsaw
Puzzle. We are all here on purpose. Please, remember
that this whole "unworthy story" is a big lie that
depression is using to try to trick you. It is not the truth.

If you need reminding of any of this, just call me.

Okay, well, let's be real: text me. I usually don't answer
my phone. (Folks living with depression will understand

that really well!

Alone Versus Lonely

"I feel lonely" is a whole different world from "I feel alone."

Lonely, as I see and feel it, is a passing phase. Lonely can be changed. Just add company: a friend, a dog, a neighbor, a phone call, any kind of reaching out. These actions may not change the circumstances. They will address the immediate issue though: the loneliness.

Feeling alone, however, is much more complex.

For those of us who walk through the darkness, we know that we can be in a room full of people – friends, family, co-workers, people we love, people we enjoy – and still feel terribly and frightfully alone.

Aloneness is internal, not external. It is not about the environment or circumstances. It is not impacted by the presence or lack of people nearby, no matter how much we may love them.

Think of it like a bruise. When we bang into something, we feel the pain of it. The bruise is the outer expression of the pain (loneliness). The injury that caused the bruise is deeper within us (aloneness).

Lonely is like the outer leaves of an artichoke.

Alone is the heart.

When I am feeling lonely, I might isolate myself. This is a choice I make.

When I feel alone, it doesn't matter if I isolate myself. It's happening anyway.

When I feel lonely, I can find ways to soothe myself. Sometimes I feed right into it and watch *The Wizard of Oz* or *Magnolia* and let myself cry until I am exhausted.

When I feel alone...there is no comfort. (Well, my dog Maddie tries her best. She offers her form of comfort.)

I have learned to navigate the world while feeling lonely as well as feeling alone.

My secret: Try not to think too much about it.

And remember how many others out there are feeling the same way.

We are, strangely, together in our aloneness.

"How Is Your Depression?"

The dilemma: Whenever I have a doctor's appointment, even just a simple checkup, I know the doctor will ask, "So, how's your depression?" I weigh my options.

First off, I want to say, "It's not 'mine.' I don't own it." That, of course, could come across as snarky and unkind. So, I defer to the next options:

1. Be honest. It's mostly manageable. Some days are worse than others. I listen to it and see what it needs to tell me.

   Result: The doctor suggests meds, which I refuse.

2. Be honest. At times, it's pretty rough. I spontaneously start crying, anywhere and anytime. I'm challenged getting out of bed in the

morning. I often feel lost and a bit hopeless. It's more of a struggle than I'd like it to be.

Result: The doctor strongly suggests meds, which I refuse. There is immediate judgment and an attitude of resignation toward my apparent stubbornness.

3. Lie. "I'm fine, everything's great."

    Result: Doctor is happy. Doctor's work here is done.

For those of us living with – and doing battle with – the darkness, choosing to - or not to - take meds is not a cavalier or whimsical decision. It is well thought out, usually based on years of dealing with sometimes crippling side effects. It is a choice based on experience, weighing the damaging impact the meds have on our bodies with the demons we face every day.

It is not stubbornness, an unwillingness to participate in our "healing," fear, an attachment to (or affection for) the depression, martyrdom, or a sign of attention-seeking.

It is a desire for some control, a desire not to feel sick or more impaired, a desire to *understand* what we're feeling as opposed to masking it, a desire for a deeper experience of all the different shades of life.

Between Two Worlds

Moments in the darkness can feel like I am living in two worlds:

The world of the "normal" people

The world of darkness

And I travel between them, back and forth.

Example: I will be driving somewhere and can easily fall into strong and painful tears. The kind of crying that comes from somewhere deep within me and cannot be soothed. And then, I arrive at my destination, Whole Foods, let's say. And I go in, shop, am friendly (genuinely), finish up, and head back to the car.

Both experiences are authentically real. And they feel like two different worlds.

One night, I went to a concert at a local outdoor venue that I've gone to since I was in my teens. I was with a longtime friend, and we were seeing an artist we had both loved "back in the day."

As I watched and listened to him perform, I was both moved to tears and lifted to my feet. I was feeling sadness and longing while also dancing and laughing – traveling back and forth from feeling to feeling.

Last night, I went to a documentary about a composer who a dear friend and I both loved. I went alone and had a "chat" with my friend before the film started. Even though he had long since graduated from Earth School, I knew that he was sitting next to me all the same.

Throughout the movie, I cried and laughed, both missing and sensing this dear man's presence.

There is happiness in the darkness.
There is depression in the appreciation.

It is not a "one or the other" experience. It is what Father Richard Rohr would call "Both and."

This is why the answer to a simple question like "So, how

are you feeling?" is such a complex challenge.

How am I feeling...?

Who I Am

So often in life, we are asked the questions "Who are you?" and "What do you do?" It's how conversations get started, how awkwardness gets dealt with, how silences get filled. It's considered "normal conversation" by most people. However, if you are someone who lives with depression, these questions can feel like indictments, like the worst test questions you could ever have to face, like the entire weight of your existence resides in whatever answer you are able to give.

I choose to use the phrase "someone who lives with depression" rather than "suffers from" because – for me – this adage rings true: "Pain is inevitable, suffering is optional." I do battle with depression; I wrestle with it, negotiate with it, argue with it, yield to it, navigate it. I do not "suffer from" it.

That said, as someone who is doing battle with depression, being asked anything about my life – my identity, what I do, who I love, how I survive, any of it –

feels laden with judgment, whether that is the intent or not. It's my perception. And it feels to me like my answer had better be great. It rarely is.

We search for "hooks" – things we can hang our purpose on – to make it look like we belong here. "I'm going to school." "I'm writing a book." "I hang out with my mom." "I volunteer at agencies that help others." I am a minister. I am a dog-mommy. I am a sister, an aunt, a great-aunt, a cousin, a niece, a daughter, a friend, a colleague, a teacher, a writer. I pray, I help, I encourage, I remind others that they're seen and heard and loved, I walk Maddie (the most amazing dog in the world), I help folks, I listen, I share...

These hooks are great. They are not really the answer that is being sought by these "party chat" questions, though. The expected answers are pithy, not deep; more specific, less complicated. They don't lead to more questions. They are asked-and-answered responses so that the questioner can move on to the next person.

Once, at a function with my mom, I was being introduced to a well-known and well-liked professor. I was excited to meet him and also was secretly dreading the "So, what do you do, Rachel?" question. Instead, he shook my hand, said how nice it was to meet me, and then he looked me directly in the eyes and asked, "So, Rachel, how do you fill your days?" I almost started crying. It was as if a light came on above us and the whole room disappeared. We had a most lovely conversation about who we actually were. And we shared long-form responses to how we each "filled our days."

It was a true gift. And I have taken his question and reused it many times, with deep Gratitude for that gift.

I've heard it said that behind every person you know is a person you don't know. We all are doing battle with one thing or another at any given moment in our lives. We are given the opportunity to engage with one another if we choose. To find out what someone is thinking about or planning. To find out about a dream or vision they have. To actually ask, "How are you feeling in your life right now?" To ask who they are, for real. And then to simply listen to their answer. To discover how they fill their days.

What a concept.

Control Is a Tool

I am writing this passage during COVID times. I was talking with a friend about the question (read as "issue") of control. How, especially during these times, control is something we all must relinquish. We simply do not have control over what is happening.

We do, of course, have control over how we handle ourselves during this time.

We can accept that it keeps us – and everyone else – safe to stay inside and follow the guidelines.

Or, we can resist those guidelines, deceiving ourselves that we have any kind of control over a virus, and put ourselves – and everyone else – at risk.

As I spoke about my own personal control issues, I talked my self right into clarity: Control is a tool. Just another one of the many tools I have in my spiritual toolbox for keeping my self alive.

Here's the thing. I have an awesome hammer in my toolbox (the one with actual tools!). It has a wood handle, it's heavy, it is very solid, and it can be used for so many things.

Except for changing a light bulb. My hammer would not be useful if I needed to change a light bulb. It also wouldn't help if I needed a screwdriver. Or any other tool in the toolbox. A hammer is useful for what hammers do.

So it is with control. I need control when I am reaching for that fourth cookie. I need control when it is garbage day and I'm feeling "just too lazy" to get it out on time.

I use control when I notice something on Facebook that I *know* will raise my cortisol if I choose to engage. I use control to scroll on by.

I use control as a tool for when I know I am faced with a situation where I must choose what is best for me, even when I do not like or agree with it.

We cannot control other people. Yes, I know. This comes as a surprise to some.

There are days when I want to step up - like *Bruce Almighty* - and take over for Spirit/God because I (big ego, I!) know that I could do a better job if I was in control of everyone and everything. This feeling happens on more days than I care to admit to, actually.

The truth is, I have control over my self, my thoughts, my choices, my own private world.

I can change my mind, convince myself of another perspective, choose better or not-so-much-better options, share my thoughts and opinions or sit quietly with them until I am feeling more clear-headed.

Giving up control – I prefer the phrase "letting loose the control" – is not a sign of weakness. It is not a surrender. It is a yielding. There is a difference.

When I yield, I choose to cooperate with what is happening and choose the best way to navigate it for my self.

In a boat, on a rafting trip in the Grand Canyon, I learned – pretty quickly – that trying to inflict my ego-centered sense of control over the Colorado River would be a magnificent failure. I had control over my own strength and resilience. The rest was about yielding to The River and working with it. Rather than trying to control it, I needed to learn how to co-operate with it. To yield to its mood and rhythm.

Not surrendering to it. Yielding to it. Co-operating with it.

When I yield, I am taking care of my self. I am using the tool of control in the way it was designed.

It can teach me. It can help me. It can keep me safe.

I'm good with that.

Empty Boat

There is a Buddhist story about a monk who wants to find a quiet place to meditate. After failing to find a quiet enough spot, he decides to get in a boat and go out onto the lake. No one else was around so he was sure he would finally be able to have some peace and quiet to meditate.

Then, out of nowhere, he feels something hit his boat. He opens his eyes – furious – and says, "Who disturbed me while I was meditating?!" He was livid that someone would crash into him like that. He was ready to really let this person have it.

The other boat, the one that had hit his, was empty.

What do we learn from this story? Well, I learned that every time I get angry at something outside of me – a person, situation, circumstance – it is not that thing that is "making" me angry. It is me doing that. Those are all just empty boats. The anger was already in me, ready at a moment's notice – or the bump of a boat – to come out, ready for a fight.

It's my reaction. Every single time.

My friend shared this story with me recently and, since then, I have put a daily reminder in my phone. Every day, at 4p, the words, "Empty Boat" appear on the home screen. And, every time I see them, I laugh out loud.

I have begun using those words as something of a rubber-band-snap-to-the-wrist kind of mantra. In traffic, while walking the dog, when the computer does something funky, whenever I feel the anger rise up – the silly anger, the un-helpful anger – I say, out loud, "Empty boat, empty boat, empty boat. Empty boat, Rachel." And I start laughing.

It was a moment like this just the other day when I realized that that other boat was not necessarily empty. I know exactly what is in that boat.

My control issues. (how many of you were not the least bit surprised by this?)

Every time the explosions of anger, the name-calling, the ridiculous self-righteous blathering would come out of me, and I would say, "Empty boat," and then laugh, I noticed that it was because I wasn't in charge of something that I felt completely capable – and totally worthy – of controlling.

Lousy drivers.
People who don't pick up after their dogs.
Rudeness.
Not returning shopping carts.
The loud noise my windshield wipers made.
Being interrupted.

As many things could be added to this list as there are moments in the day.

A hair clip fell out of my hair as I was removing my hat. I couldn't find it. It was stupid, AND, it was a last-straw-moment after several other annoyances had been building up. And as I got ready to scream about it, I said, "WOW! That is a seriously empty boat, Rachel."

During a season of quarantine, holidays, pressure, weather, isolation, change, and whatever else can be tossed into the basket of this December, it seems that in a strange way, I am going to have to pay extra attention to when I seem to be tethering my boat to that empty boat (that is not as empty as I thought).

So attached to wanting things to "be easier" or "run smoother" or be less of all of those things I listed. The more I hold onto the rope that connects me to that empty boat, the less attention I am paying to my own boat (which, at times, needs serious attention!!).

My boat could use some patching up. Some bailing.

Some fresh paint.

Some Kindness.

Ah....If my boat could hold a bit more Kindness - to myself and to others - that empty boat would just float on by and away out into the ocean.

I think I just discovered my New Year's Intention.

Make next year: Empty Boat Release Year.

To Tell the Truth

When I am honest...

some people don't want to hear it

some want to change it

some want to fix it

some want to interpret it (to make sense for themselves, I suppose) some interpret it incorrectly

some judge me for my truth

some regret asking me to be honest

some take on what I've said as their own burden

some get hurt

some choose to leave

it helps me

it hurts me

it brings some closer

it moves some away

it clarifies

it confuses

it's always worth it

it's always terrifying

it's what people want

it's absolutely what people do *not* want

it can be a wonderful surprise

it feels like a triumph

it feels like a loss

it's never a draw.

The Chasm

There was a time not so long ago when I thought I had beaten the depression – I had gotten past it, gotten over it, was done with it. It was amazing. I had never believed I could get to that point.

Up until that time, the depression had been a demon, an entity that haunted and tormented me. It mocked my efforts, always reminding me that I belonged to it and would never be free. It was like the worst roommate I could ever have: disrespectful of my time and space, usurping my energy, leaving its mess everywhere around me, encouraging me to do nothing.

And then, things changed. In my thirties, I moved from my hometown in Ohio to Alaska, and my spiritual journey became a much more serious endeavor, one with focus and a goal. The constant hum of depression became very quiet, like it was confused by who I was becoming. This was lovely for quite a while.

I wrote and performed a show about overcoming depression. I became a role model for recovery. I was convinced that the depression was gone, left somewhere far behind me.

Then a moment came when I started feeling the metaphorical ground crumbling under my feet. I lost two of my closest friends in less than three months. I was in a relationship at the time, and it came to a cruel and startling end. I turned around and realized that the depression wasn't far behind me at all. It was, in fact, right behind me, and I was on the edge of an abyss, a deep chasm. I was losing ground and was at imminent risk of sliding down into it.

I was working at the time with an amazing therapist named Sarah. She asked me what I was seeing as I imagined this visual. I described it like the Grand Canyon, and I was standing on the rim, feeling the earth dissolving under my shoes, and falling backward, losing ground and slipping down, all the way down, into the depths of the darkness.

She suggested that I add a couple of things to this visual: Trees, shrubs, or rocks – something that I could grab onto to stop me from sliding.

Switchbacks and a path, so that it wasn't a direct unstoppable slide downward.

With these things to help grab onto, I wouldn't end up so far into the chasm that I couldn't get back up from it. And, when I did start falling, there would be places where I could stop or at least slow myself down. They could help make climbing back up and out not quite so difficult.

I found these visuals immensely helpful. They took the panic out of the moments of slippage and removed the sense of failure I often felt when I started to fall. They allowed me to accept that it was okay to believe that I had moved past depression, and that it was also okay that it had been right behind me all along.

I no longer believe it's possible or even necessary to live completely free from the depression. I don't need to be healed from it. I do need to remember that every time I have slid down into the chasm, I have managed to climb back out.

My success rate for surviving so far is one hundred percent.

Notes to Self on How to Respond to Depression

What Not to Do:
- Listen to the Knight of the Mirrors
- Stay up past a normal bedtime
- Purposefully watch movies/TV shows that will spiral me downward
- Stop showering
- Punish myself for not doing enough
- Compare myself with others
- Obsess on anxiety symptoms as if they're heart attack symptoms

- Eat "just because"
- Avoid contact with people
- Overwhelm myself with thinking about all of the stuff I "must" get done
- Give up (which is different from yielding – there is a difference)
- Obsess on what has been or what cannot be
- Punish myself for asking for or needing support
- Let small issues become large ones (Empty Boat!)
- Minimize the things I actually get done
[a] Purchase or eat ready-to-spread frosting (the canary-in-the-coal-mine warning that things have gotten out of control!)

What to Do:
- Re: ready-to-spread frosting: praise myself for resisting the urge to buy/eat it
- Open the shades
- Set an alarm
- Take meds/vitamins
- Create a to-do list of small, easy-to-tackle tasks
- Eat healthy food at normal intervals
- Brush AND floss, EVERY day
- Put on a bra, at least every once in a while, especially when leaving the house

- Accept invitations to do things (be gentle with myself on this one)
- Read
- Reach out/offer support to others (even a "hello" text)
- Write (letters, journal, e-mails, anything)
- Deal with challenges one small step at a time
- Ask for help
- Be gentle with myself (a recurring theme)
- Make lists
- Acknowledge every step, no matter how small
- Throw the ball (Maddie taught me this one)
- Say out loud what I am grateful for; scream it if I want
- Hydrate

These might seem basic to some people. To those of us who are walking, living, breathing, and moving through the darkness, these are epic things. Knowing upon waking that I won't see anyone all day is NOT an excuse to not brush and floss my teeth, or to not shower. And. At the same time, there are days when it is simply too hard to do any of these things. Learning to balance my own judgment around this, and not punishing myself when I miss the mark, is key to taking care of myself.

Sitting

The dangers of sitting down while depressed are many.
The most treacherous of the dangers is this: Once sitting,
it is nearly impossible to get back up again.
There are so many good reasons not to move:

There's always one more game of solitaire to play on my
phone.

And one more pass through the Facebook newsfeed.

Maddie is sleeping on me, so...(This reason is legitimate.)

It's cloudy outside, and I'm watching the wind blow
through the trees.

I fell asleep.

And on and on...and on and on....

When I am up and moving, so much gets done:

laundry

dishes

kitchen counters get cleared

clothes get washed, sorted, and put away

projects get completed

And then...I sit down.

It's as if life gets a chance to catch up to me when I sit down. And in come the waves

of sad

of lonely

of left

of missing

of hurt

of lost

of loss

And an hour has passed..

How Are You Dealing With....

The latest catastrophe? The most recent celebrity suicide? That breakup? That diagnosis? That loss? That change?

I have come to learn that this darkness within me has little to do with what is going on around me. I don't always respond to sad news with a bout of depression. And I sometimes slide down into the abyss when everything seems to be going fine.

So, what is it then?

My experience of depression is internal, volcanic, within me.

It is not affected by the outer world, outer happenings, appearances, etc.

"What's going on?" It doesn't matter.

What happens "out there" might be the flint that the

match strikes...still, the match is in me.

What can I do about that?
Find an anchor to keep me from drifting.

Rely on spiritual practices (of whatever kind, no rules, no limitations).

Find a reason to get out of bed each day (having a pet really helps with this).

Find one way to step outside of myself, just one way (volunteering: Meals on Wheels, pick up garbage in our neighborhood, read to the elderly, plant in a community garden, sing to shelter animals, hold babies at the hospital...)

Sit quietly somewhere to watch life unfolding (in the park, at the zoo...)

It may not be easy. It might feel uncomfortable. It might be painful (physically or otherwise). It might seem scary. It might feel completely impossible.

It's okay. I can feel all of that. And then, when I'm ready:

Do. One. Thing.

Living With

Living with depression is just that: *Living WITH* it.

Just like any other chronic condition, it is not about the suffering or the struggling or the victimization. It is about the *Living with*.

Waking up every day. Taking a moment to be Grateful for another chance. Assessing how much energy I have for the day. Taking a moment to stretch and breathe deeply so that oxygen can reach the parts of my body that are experiencing pain. Drinking a glass of water to hydrate myself. And doing each little act that so many take for granted:

Brush my teeth.

Take a shower.

Eat something (even a Girl Scout cookie counts as breakfast on some days).

Walk my Maddie.

Living with the experience is accepting that – in this moment – it is what is happening. Denying, hiding, pretending do not serve me. Believing that it will last forever does not serve me.

I have watched friends make fruitless attempts at trying to force the depression away. They take meds (without doing any introspective, therapeutic, or spiritual work, simply expecting them to 'fix' it). They eat obsessively. They drink alcohol. They go from romantic relationship to romantic relationship, creating stories of how love can save them without ever being fully invested in or honest about those relationships.

I have watched myself retreat into isolation. I have become overwhelmingly dependent on my dog for support and comfort. I have enough Girl Scout cookies in my freezer to survive a zombie apocalypse. I have tried to hide from Spirit/God (as I understand It), thinking that I can "manage" this on my own.

And what it always comes back to is this question: How do I want to live?

I find that when I allow the depression to keep me in bed or hold me down or back, I am letting the depression run my life. I am letting it run me. I am letting the story of depression become my story. And I cannot do that.

I have tried to outrun it, to deny it, to pretend I am "fine." This is unsustainable; it takes way more energy than I could ever muster. So, I cannot do that either.

One big lesson that I have learned is this: The depression needs to be heard and acknowledged. When every part of me, inside and out, is calling for quiet, begging for a nap, demanding time in my "cave," I must honor that message. If I try to ignore it, I struggle.

To *Live with* is to be patient. To Listen to myself. To accept where I am in each given moment. To forgive the moments of slippage that happen from time to time. To remain courageous in the face of what frightens me. To speak authentically about what is happening within me.

And to show up, every day. Grateful for another chance to stretch, breathe, and try again.

Notes for Others on How to Respond to Depression

I was thinking recently about things that people have said to me while I was in a dark space — things that helped, and things that didn't.

<u>What It Helps Me to Hear:</u>

I'll follow your lead. If you're able to, please let me know what you need.

Would you like to sit outside for a little bit, get some fresh air?

Want to take a short walk?

Is there anything I can do?

Would talking help?

You've been doing really well.

I'm here if you need me.

It's okay to feel what you're feeling. I'm just concerned for your safety.

What have you done in the past that's helped?

<u>What Doesn't Help:</u>

Why don't you just DO something? Sitting around isn't good for you.
Just get over it.
Move on. I mean, seriously.
You always do this to yourself. Stop it.
You're not going to do something stupid, are you?
Go to the gym. Moving around will get you out of the dumps.
Why don't you call someone? You never ask for help.
Oh. THIS, again.
You're never going to meet anyone if you keep this up.
And the dreaded "shoulds":

> You *should* go for a walk
> You *should* exercise
> You *should* see a therapist
> You *should* take meds
> You *should* do something
> You *should* know better

When I was in the psych unit in NYC, I remember trying to explain how challenging it is to understand this experience. When someone has cancer or a broken leg or some kind of tangible medical affliction, it's easier to

127

explain. Easier to understand. And, of course, I am not belittling anyone's personal medical nightmare. The comparison is one of visible versus invisible.

We can see someone hurting physically. We understand that cancer is bad, that a broken bone is painful, that physical illnesses are uncomfortable and scary and can be financially terrifying. We know what to do with those situations. And saying something unhelpful is less likely, because it's easier to have compassion for someone who is suffering from something we can see.

When someone is hurting internally, psychologically, emotionally, spiritually, it becomes a whole different scenario. Things that are said – well-meaning things – are cruel and hurtful. "Get off your pity pot." "Why don't you just get dressed and go DO something?" "Why do you continue to mope?" "Do you know how many people have it worse than you?"

The thing is, very few people really *want* to see it, deal with it, talk about it. After all, it's exhausting. When I was in the hospital, people would come to visit me and not know what to say. We would just sit there awkwardly for the obligatory amount of time that made it seem like they really wanted to be there, and then they would feel it was okay to leave. I don't say this ungratefully; I say it honestly. I was not easy to be around, especially those last couple weeks of 1987. I couldn't entertain people or even come up with things to talk about, so the encounters were strange, surreal, uncomfortable.

When I could fake it, folks felt more at ease. And I wanted them to feel that way. So, I would fake it. I am really quite skilled at that. It's just that the damage done to me from faking it would be something I would have to deal with later on, by myself. Like attacks on my soul, those post-faking-it moments were vicious.

People didn't see that. Most people don't see what the true experience is like for a person living with chronic severe depression. They see the outer trappings of it, which also look like laziness or not even trying. When we have the strength to pull ourselves together enough to be social, the immediate response is often "Look at you! You're BACK! You're doing so much better! Good to see you're over all of that." And we smile and nod and don't respond because, if we try, the tears will start and we'll have to run away like Cinderella, leaving our dignity like a glass shoe behind us.

We don't "get over it." It doesn't go away or stop or get

fixed. No medication cures it, although some might help or appear to help. (What they also might do is cause us to feel sleepy, give us liver damage and hand tremors, and make us fat. Not so helpful.) It is a process, every day, every breath, every moment. A process.

Today, after staying up too late last night, doing many things on my what-not-to-do list, I got out of bed. I brushed and flossed. I washed my hair. I put on a bra. I dispatched a spider. (Have I mentioned I cannot cohabitate with spiders?) I took care of my beloved dog Maddie's needs. I checked online job postings. I wrote. I met a friend for lunch. And, up until this very moment, I hadn't cried. (I made it a little over two hours. I consider that a good day.)

JIMMY AND CARL
AND MICHAEL AND ME

Where I keep my self....Where I give my self
What I share and what I hide away
It's all a part....it's all because
I thought the ones who would stay,
were the ones who went away

~ rev rachel hollander, Today

So we live and we learn
But we only learn if we live

~ Michael Devon

The Dearly Departed

To know me means to know that I have many dead friends. I want to share about three of those friends whose absence I feel every single day: Jimmy, Carl, and Michael. I feel it's important to tell you a bit about them. They're so much a part of my story.

Jimmy

Jimmy was my soul twin. From the moment we met in 1991, doing a community theatre show together, we somehow knew that we were not meeting for the first time. There were so many ways we were connected; we understood each other so deeply and felt each other's pain so honestly. After years of the tightest connection, we had an excruciating falling out that I still don't understand. It led to two years of silence between us. I grieved the loss of my friend, who I missed so much.

Early in 2013, I reached out to him, and we had a brief moment of reconnection. I didn't push for more – I was too afraid to, though I can't explain why. In May that year, he died in his sleep at age forty-nine. Completely unexpected. It was then that the real grieving began, because there was never going to be another opportunity for reaching out – for anything.

In recognition of my own fear, and in honor of Jimmy, I had this Spanish proverb tattooed on my forearm, so I would never let fear stop me again: *Vivir con miedo es como vivir a medias* (A life lived in fear is a life half-lived). I hope to see Jimmy again in our next incarnation, when we can sit together and work it all out. Until that reunion happens, though, I know he's always with me.

Carl

In 1983, I was hired to work an office gig at a video distributor. It was instantly clear that this was not the right job for me. I was unlike everyone else there and simply didn't fit in. A woman there said, "You should really meet my husband. You two would definitely be friends." That's how I met Carl. Through the years, we rescued, supported, listened to, and argued with each other. Through disasters and crises, both large and small, we were always there for each other. He was like a big brother to me. I loved him with all of my heart. He visited me twice while I lived in Alaska and wanted so very much to live there.

Only a few days after Jimmy's funeral, Carl told me that he was diagnosed with cancer. He had only a few months left. We chatted on the phone weekly, and I was sure that he knew how much I loved him. He left the planet just under three months after Jimmy. I miss Carl every day.

Michael

Michael was a brilliant writer and composer. He was sharp, sensitive, hilariously funny, and tragically self-deprecating. He was a light in this world. We met when I lived in NYC in the mid-1980s. At that time, he was creating a musical theatre piece based on the Gail Parent novel *Sheila Levine is Dead and Living in New York*, the painful and funny story of an overweight woman finding her way to her own self-identity – and to love – in NYC in the early 1970s. The show reflected Michael in many ways, and as we would come to discover, it was my experience as well. We would spend hours in his apartment, crying, eating pound cake, and drinking lemonade. And then, after all of that, he'd make me sing! I was so honored to be part of his project and in his circle.

When I left NYC, we wrote "snail mail" letters to each other for the next three years, up until his death. We helped each other, encouraged each other, and made each other laugh and sometimes cry. After he was gone, I had our letters bound into a book, and I read them whenever I need to hear his voice cheering me up and telling me to keep going. I'm grateful for technology that allows me to have recordings of our sessions together so I can listen to – and sing along with – the brilliant original score that Michael created.

Michael's "Questions for Rachel"

When I was in my deep sadness while living in NYC, Michael chided me for not picking myself up and getting better. He said some of the very things I now encourage other people to never say to someone who is depressed. He loved me – I knew that. He just didn't understand my experience. A few years later, Michael himself became very ill. His body was betraying him, and he had slipped into an isolating depression.

Michael sent me a long list of questions with the genuine desire for answers about depression. At the time, I didn't have any good answers to offer him. I do now, though. And somehow, I know he knows. These questions so clearly reflect the thoughts of someone doing battle with the darkness.

1. Onset of symptoms – what symptoms were there – what, if anything, triggered them? Reactive or endogenous depression?

2. Worst time of day? Did you feel any better at night? Was it difficult getting up in the morning?

3. Did you blame yourself for your depression? Did you feel like it was something inadequate about you?

4. Did it steadily worsen over time or was it about the same? Any suicidal ideation? Did you think about ways to do it? If so, did that increase over time?

5. Did it ever stop, even for an hour? Were there times when you were able to forget it? Initial coping strategies (before hospital)?

6. Did you have a hard time making decisions? Getting anything done? Forgetful? Did you tire easily?

7. How did you look at your future? Were you scared?

8. Describe life in the hospital. What therapeutic steps did they take? Was it any relief to be around people who understood what you were going through?

9. Drugs. Did they help? How long did they take to work? Which were you on? Did they ever make you feel better? Which ones?

10. Describe ECT. Do you think it worked?

11. When and how did the depression end? (Or did it?)

12. Did you have any coping strategies? Was it difficult being around people? Did you find yourself getting more and more isolated? Was it difficult or embarrassing to talk about it?

13. What was the most painful, or three of the most painful things about the depression?

These were only some of the questions that Michael asked me.

As I read over all of his questions, thinking back on when he wrote them, what was happening with him at that time, what was happening with me at that time, and what is happening to me now, so many years later, I can't stop the millions of different feelings from flooding in.

When he sent those questions to me, it was because he was slipping into a really deep darkness, quite possibly the last of his life. And he was reaching out to me for answers because I seemed to have "gotten through" or "gotten past" the depression. He looked to me as a guide, as a light on the path ahead of him, as someone who knew something, who had some answers.

At this point in time, he was feeling bad for the things he had said to me when I was in the hospital. Back then, when I was losing the battle with the darkness, he was so frustrated with me. He was always saying cliché comments that hurt so much: *Get over it, go take a walk, get off your pity pot, just stop it.* He was impatient with me. Or, at least, he seemed to be.

In retrospect, it was clear that he was afraid. What was happening to me scared him because he knew it could happen to him. He and I were so much alike, that fear was sharp and real.

When we got to the point of him sending me those questions, Michael was struggling with his body breaking down due to complications from a dreadful disease. He shared with me that others were now saying to him all of those clichés that he had said to me. He was realizing how much they stung, and he apologized to me for having said them. There were very few – if any – people he could trust to ask these questions who wouldn't immediately assume he was considering suicide. He was not. At that moment, he was fighting to stay alive amidst the biggest challenge he had ever faced. He knew he could ask me. And he knew that I would answer honestly, just as I'm trying to do on these pages.

New Year's Eve

New Year's Eve has always been one of the most challenging nights for me. Back when I was younger, it was the night that I would reevaluate whether or not I would "stay" for more. When I was thirteen, I promised myself that, if I wanted to, I could remove myself from this life on the New Year's Eve of the year I reached thirty.

On New Year's Eve 1994, my sweet friend Amy was killed in New Orleans. She was thirty-one years old and was destroyed by a bullet descending after someone had aimed celebratory shots into the air.

Jimmy used to help me get through this night with laughter and movies and crying. Lots of each.

Movies are very special to me, and they were to Jimmy as well. Every New Year's Eve, I now watch *The Poseidon Adventure* (one of our favorites). I still laugh at that silly Red Buttons moment after Shelley Winters dies. This year, I swore I could hear Jimmy laughing with me. I laughed even as I was crying.

Truly, Madly, Deeply with Alan Rickman...*American Beauty*...*The Last Temptation of Christ*...*Magnolia*...*True Romance* – movies were one of the many ways Jimmy and I connected with each other. Movies and pizza and tears and laughter.

Each New Year's Eve, I hold a vision that we will all have more love, more passion, more healing, more possibility, more commitment, more meaning, and more happiness than we have experienced in past years.

If only we could bring our loved ones back to share it all with us.

The Other Shoe

There are times when I find myself sinking into anxiety, into worry. Especially when things are going well (whatever that actually means), moments when it feels like life is safe and I can relax.

I start waiting. I stop taking deep breaths. What am I waiting for? I am waiting for the other shoe to drop:

the next death

the next hurt

the next horrible thing

the next disappointment

The moment of discovering that I've been lied to. The next betrayal.

I can feel my chest tighten. I can feel myself preparing for it. I sit and wait in anticipation of the next thing that's going to hurt me because – and this is where the danger lies – I feel sure that it's always going to come.

I have been taught to "live in the moment." I know what that means.

I have practiced deconstructing the mental noise that confounds and attempts to derail me. I know how to do this.

I live a daily Practice of Gratitude, for everything in every moment. I know the importance of this.

And with all of those – and so many more – tools in my toolbox, I still find myself filling with fear, shaking with anxiety, paralyzed by the knowledge that "something bad" is going to happen at any moment. And that there's nothing I can do about it.

I remind myself in those moments that there is *always* something I can do about it.

No matter what the Knights or the demons or the darkness try to tell me, my Mind is mine to steer. And I continue to recalibrate my compass and redirect my course.

Jimmy Wisdom

Jimmy once wrote this to me: "Dealing with depression is like a house of cards that you have to rebuild every day. Sometimes the cards are just a little slippery." Jimmy truly understood this experience – and me – really well.

"Recovering" from depression, by which I mean learning to live with, manage, tolerate, and integrate it, is such a fragile process. I try not to get overconfident or egotistical about it. That happened to me, accidentally, several years ago. I felt like I had conquered the depression, that it was all behind me, and that I could talk about it in the past tense. I learned.

Back in the days when the depression felt like a house of cards, made with slippery cards, I had few tools to slow my descent – no switchbacks to make the path less straight and steep, and nothing to hold onto. The fall was quick and mean. I would wake up on my back at the base of the abyss, wondering what happened and whether I could recover from it. No tools. Nothing to grab onto.

And when – or if – I would call out for help, I would hear only the echo of my own voice. I couldn't appreciate anything around me, even the smallest of things. No gratitude. No trust. Alone.

These days, the difference is mighty. The switchbacks I've designed keep me from sliding all the way down. The rocks and trees I have installed give me something to grab onto. And I do grab. I stop myself the best I can. I don't want to slide to the bottom. I want to save myself, as much as I am able to.

When I call out for help – and I do, now – there are people who hear me, who don't try to fix it (or me). They patiently try to understand, ask what I need, and allow me the space to not know what I need.

I have some tools now. The cards don't always seem quite so slippery.

Then again, I've also learned that tools don't always help. As someone who has studied, been in therapy, walked this path many times, read up, helped others, been in the depths of the darkness, and also walked in the light of inner peace, I can honestly say none of that may matter when the tsunami-like wave of pain, sadness, and darkness returns.

And it does return. That we can be sure of, those of us who have lived this reality. It doesn't just go away and stay away. It ebbs and flows on its own, or sometimes it can be brought on by external situations: frustrations, lack of communication, disappointments, obstacles, change, loss.

And knowing what is causing it, knowing what it is, knowing what has worked before, knowing what to do...sometimes none of that matters one bit.
That's when you sit down. Breathe. Cry. And remember that it has come before and it has left before...
Remember.

Vanish

Around 9:00 p.m. on Wednesday, September 17, 1975, my dad's heart gave up working. It stopped, dramatically, in the midst of a tennis game. The people at the tennis courts, the Emergency Technicians, the doctors, nurses, and his tennis partner, they all saw him as – and after – his soul left his body.

For me, he vanished.

I was told what happened, told he had died. I was never shown his body (because he did not look like himself anymore and, being twelve, I did not need that image of him to be the lasting one). He was, basically, gone. Vanished.

Since then, there have been others I have loved who have vanished in similar ways: Marc, Amy, Jimmy, Michael, Carl, too many. I loved them, they loved me, we were essential in and to each other's lives. And...gone. Vanished. I have lost them.

There's a difference between losing a pen or a lip balm or that matching sock and losing a person or a pet or a memory. There are things that we – okay, I – can handle losing and there are things that, once lost, leave a hole that can never be filled.

When someone vanishes, it disturbs me. It feels incomplete, unfair. Why did they go? Where did they go? Will I ever see them again? What about all of those things I want to tell them?

There is unfinished business that can never be finished. The pen, the lip balm, the sock, all of these have the potential to be found or replaced. A person cannot be...well, at least not in the form that we knew them.

In my experience with death, it has almost always been a sudden loss. No dramatic languishing, long goodbyes, singing at the bedside, making plans for what needs to happen next. None of that. Just...gone. Vanished. Like a really sick and unpleasant magic trick: They are there one moment and then, poof, gone.

That is the distinction for me between vanishing and leaving. When someone leaves, there is the possibility for closure, for a farewell, for the potential of understanding, for a sense of gentleness. When someone vanishes, it is like a jolt, like being rear-ended in your car while you're changing the radio station. Sudden, sharp, disturbing. Uncomfortable.

That is it: There is no comfort in someone (or something) vanishing. It feels more like something has been taken rather than lost. There is a mysterious element to it. A frustrating element, even.

"I put that book on the table, and now it seems to have vanished."

"I was just using my phone – it has vanished."

"We had plans to have tea on Thursday..."

Now I understand more why I like to have my "Guardian Wall" altar in my home. When I see my friends, when I can look at them and feel their presence, it feels less like they have vanished and more like they have simply moved into another realm.

There are conversations that we cannot actually have, forgiveness that can never be fully granted, hugs that will never be felt again. Those opportunities have vanished along with the bodies of these people. However, their souls will never disappear, their souls will never vanish.

> "To live in hearts we leave behind is not to die."
> –Thomas Campbell

From Tears of Grief to Tears of Gratitude

For many years I lived in Cleveland, Ohio. All over it: East, West, South, from Shaker Heights to Richmond Heights to Cleveland Heights to Old Brooklyn to Lakewood to Ohio City and more. I moved a lot. (A LOT!)

Over the course of twelve years, I think I moved at least fourteen times. And each time I moved I always had a group of people to help me. These included friends, co-workers, castmates...so many wonderful folks from all the different areas of my life. They would come together and lug all of my stuff (and there was a lot of stuff, including a small piano) up and down stairs, through small doorways, into trucks and cars and whatever vehicles we could gather together.

Always, at every one of these moves, there were three gentlemen who I called "My Boys": Carl, Jimmy, and John. They were the three I could always rely on, always call, always trust. Not only when I needed to move, though. They were the three people who I could trust with my life.

I had met Carl back in 1983. We shared music, we talked about all kinds of topics, we'd stay up late just hanging out, and he'd take me for rides on his motorcycle. He even rescued a box of eight-track tapes from a dumpster for me!

Jimmy came next. 1991. We were both cast in a community theatre production of *Jesus Christ Superstar*. That first night we met, we started trying to figure out where we knew each other from. There seemed to be no place or time that our lives had intersected, and yet the connection between us was instantly strong and felt like it had always been there. Three different psychics told us that we had known each other over the course of many lifetimes, that we just kept finding one another. We were soul twins. We felt that, knew it, right away.

And then came John. 1992. I placed a personal ad in the newspaper. Something like: "Dagny Taggart wanna-be seeking Hank Rearden type for conversation and..." I can't remember the rest. I had just read *Atlas Shrugged* and was inspired. He answered it, we met for lunch, we found one another interesting. On our first dinner date, about a week later, the server asked us what anniversary we were celebrating. When we said that it was just our second date, she commented, "Wow, you two just seem so comfortable with each other, I thought you'd been together a while." We realized fairly early on that we were much better as friends than anything more than that. And yet, we have always been so much more than "just" friends. He is another brother. Always honest, always snarky. And truly the best chef I have ever met.

When I moved away from Ohio in 2000, that last time, they all (except for Carl, he refused to help with that move!) had to cart the piano down a flight of stairs. We all laughed that this was THE LAST time they would ever help me move! I was moving to Alaska, so that was a pretty accurate statement! Jimmy made the drive with me across the country and up to my new home in Anchorage.

All three of them, at different times, came to see me in Alaska. Carl even talked about moving there. I missed them all very much when I lived there and was so Grateful for the e-mails and phone calls that kept our connection solid. When I would come "home" to Cleveland, we would always get together and laugh and share stories.

Over the years, there were "falling-out" moments with each of My Boys. Times when we disagreed or hurt each other. Choices we made that caused each other to feel forgotten. There would be some periods of silence. We would always come back around, though. Well, almost always.

In May of 2013, I got the call that Jimmy had died in his sleep. At forty-nine years of age, he was just...gone. About three months later, Carl left at age fifty-two. I was four-thousand miles away physically. I was right there with them emotionally. When I talked to John, he joked, in his sweet yet edgy way, "Well, I'M still alive."

Fast forward.

I moved back to Cleveland in 2016 and was living in a great place that – after two years – became problematic. I spent ten months looking for a new home and finally found it. Which meant I had to move.

I had done a few moves after leaving Ohio in 2000. I had become a much more efficient and organized mover. And I had managed to cultivate wonderful friends who always offered to help. So, I hadn't really missed not having My Boys with me.

Now, I was here. Back in Ohio. Moving. Without My Boys. (Back in 2000, John was one of the loudest voices saying he would NEVER help me move again.) So, I hired movers, and I packed everything and was ready for the big day. Almost.

The night before the move, I had a meltdown. I realized that I was one vehicle short of full coverage. There were things that the movers wouldn't take (open bags of stuff, odd-shaped items that didn't go into boxes, etc.). My car was full. I needed help.

I am not very good at asking for help. What most people hear when they ask me if I need anything is, "I'm good. I've got this. Don't need anything." And they believe me.

At 2:00 a.m. of moving day, I needed help. And it felt like there was no one there.

The grief hit hard, and it hit strong. Six years dissolved into the moment I first got those calls that Jimmy and Carl had died. They were truly gone. They were never coming back. I didn't have My Boys. I was alone.

I curled up into a ball and let the darkness take over. Usually, I put up a pretty decent fight. There was no fighting it now; this battle was lost before it began. I missed them. It became much more real: their absence, what they meant in my life, how much I needed them, how much I counted on them being there. It had never fully hit me how they could simply not be here. The grief was overwhelming.

And then, within a few hours, the miracles started happening.

My mom called and asked if she could help. A friend from high school who I hadn't seen in years reached out through Facebook with a message that simply said, "Do you need help?" Friends came and brought food. They assembled – and made – my bed so I would be able to go right to sleep that night. There were messages of support, prayers being spoken, and so much Love. Just...so much Love.

Within twenty-four hours, my tears of grief had transformed into tears of Gratitude.

It is okay to grieve. It is okay to miss them every day. It is okay to wish that they were still here. Because they ARE still here. I see them in photos and mementos. I hear them in memory. I feel them comforting me. I know, now, that they will never leave me.

I feel the Presence of Jimmy and Carl, laughing and smiling and celebrating with me in this new home.

Oh, and John – the "last one standing" – made me an awesome clock for my living room.

My Boys live on.

On the Move

I spent the first twenty years of my life in one house, the Fortress (I called it) on Rye Road. I think, in some ways, I imagined that I would never leave that house. That nothing would ever change and I would always live there.

That September night in 1975 changed the story. It also changed me.

There's an early childhood developmental theory called Object Permanence. It is the stage of learning that teaches toddlers that just because they don't see something anymore, that doesn't mean it is completely gone. Like, their jar of baby food in the cupboard. That's why we play "peek-a-boo." We are teaching this essential concept.

The night my Dad died, even though I was twelve, I regressed. Somehow, my Object Permanence connection was cut. And from that night on, the sense of "nothing lasting" became the unconscious motivation behind every decision I made.

Relationships, housing, employment, my life. Even my life

seemed to be something I couldn't rely on. Things disappear. People disappear. Sometimes it feels like I disappear.

After the hospital, after I was told that I would have to live in a group home taking meds the rest of my life, I considered that option. I thought about how easy it would be. How, eventually, those who loved me would stop visiting (because, of course, nothing lasts), and how it would make total sense living there because people (staff, other "patients") would come and go. Just like everything else.

I eventually moved into an apartment. And then another one. And then I was briefly engaged and moved into a house. Then, to someone else's house (after I left the engagement). And then another and another and another. And then another state. And another and another and another.

The doctors at the hospital said that I had no organizational skills.

Their minds would be blown if they could see me move.

I have mastered the art of looking for, looking at, and

choosing places to live. I can pack boxes by room, theme, importance, or weight.

My list of "to-do's" is meticulous (utilities, address changes, driver's license, etc.).

There may still be days when I can't get out of bed or can't stop crying. In fact, there *are* still days like that. However, when it comes to moving, Object Permanence and I have come to an understanding.

Patience

Having companions in the darkness helps to find the patience required to face the avalanche of well-meaning yet hurtful questions and suggestions seemingly hurled at us without any awareness of their impact. Losing companions, ones who understood this so deeply, makes having no response to these questions and suggestions so much more painful.

"Don't you even want to get better? It sure doesn't seem like it."

"What are you doing to try harder?"

"Why do you buy into those false beliefs? You know better."

"You have so much more than others do. I mean, you don't live in Syria. What do you have to be depressed about?"

"I thought you were 'so grateful' all the time. You don't seem very grateful."

"Maybe if you lost some weight, you'd feel better."

"You should socialize more, stop isolating."

"Why don't you take meds? If they help, why do you refuse to take them?"

There are answers to each of these. If it wasn't so very exhausting to provide those answers, we would.

Isn't it enough that we are here, trying, showing up, giving what we can, taking up as little space as we are able to, trying not to cause a stir or draw attention?

If we only breathe deeply and seem to sigh, it's because our answers can feel so futile.

And, in order to answer, we have to climb up from the deep well of judgment and shame that these questions and statements bury us in.

"You should date."

"You should definitely not date."

"How will you ever meet someone if you don't cheer up?"

"You are in no position to be in a relationship. You're kind of exhausting."

"So, when does this change? I mean, when does it stop?"
"You were laughing yesterday, I thought you were all better."

"My cousin/sister/nephew/uncle/college roommate/co-worker has depression. I know all about it."

If our responses aren't enough, please know this: we are being patient with you.

Please be patient with us.

HIGH RESOLVE

The Voice that Calls to me comes from within
It tells me where I stand
Time to begin
I Listen and I hear it
Accepting what's revealed
As I get still I learn how to Live, to See, to Be

I Know I'm Guided
I Know I'm shown which way to go
I Know I'm Guided
And all I need to know
I Know

~ rev rachel hollander, assisi

Me and Brother Francesco – 1972-2009 (and beyond)

At the age of nine, I was taken to see the film *Brother Sun, Sister Moon*. It is a gorgeous Franco Zeffirelli-directed film about the early life and spiritual revelation of Saint Francis of Assisi, or as I like to call him, Brother Francesco. As the final credits rolled, that first time seeing it, I couldn't stop the tears from flowing. My Mom asked me what was wrong, and all I could say was, "I want to go be with him, I belong with him." Her response was hilariously predictable: 1. I was Jewish. 2. He was dead. 3. I was a girl!

From that moment, though, I knew that in some past life I must have walked with Brother Francesco. I felt a powerful kinship with him, with his connection to Spirit, with his rejection of "traditional religion" (and all of its limitations and rules and exclusionary practices), and with his sense of Oneness with all beings, human and animal. He was always much more to me than "the patron saint of animals." He heard a clear message from God/Spirit and listened to it, without question. And this listening brought him peace and purpose.

Throughout my life, Brother Francesco has been a guiding influence for me. He is a member of what I call "My Soul Team," which also includes Joan of Arc, Don Quixote, Mother Teresa, Vincent van Gogh, Brother Lawrence, Sister Teresa of Ávila...His prayers, his way of being, his transformation and life have taught me so much about how I want to walk in my life.

I especially feel his presence with me when the darkness moves in. It helps me to know that he had moments in the darkness as well, moments when he felt defeated and lost. I think about him climbing Mount Subasio, sitting in his cave, crying, singing, and listening to the rain.

Wanting to sit in that cave and listen to what he heard was one of the motivations for my trip of a lifetime: a sojourn to Assisi in 2009. Finally, thirty-six years after that movie moment, I was going to walk in his steps and breathe his air.

Yes, Assisi is something of a tourist town (the number of buses arriving each day was impressive!), and it was filled with T-shirts and statuettes and images and icons of this man. And yet I always remembered this: there are Holy places, and their Holiness meets us at the door. We bring some of their Holiness in with us. So, I found a way to make all those people – all that noise and consumerism – vanish from my experience as I brought my Holy to The Holy, as I focused only on my vision and my mission. For me, this was a pilgrimage. Nothing else mattered.

Spirit was with me the entire time, everywhere I walked; I never felt alone. There are three moments that stand out in particular.

The day I walked down to San Damiano – September 17 – was not only my dad's thirty-fourth yahrzeit (the anniversary of his "graduation from Earth School"), it was also the date when people commemorate Brother Francesco receiving the stigmata (his hands and feet spontaneously bled where Jesus' wounds were). It felt like a day filled with powerful energy. I could feel my dad walking with me down the path, past the signs that requested total silence and respect for the surroundings. I felt him every time I heard the bells. San Damiano is still an active spiritual home, so visitors can see it only briefly, and then the grounds are closed for sacred prayer time. I found a low stone wall nearby to sit on, have a small picnic, journal, and look out over the valley, seeing "new town" Assisi and the very large church (St. Mary of the Angels) inside which the Brother's small home - the Portiuncula - was preserved.

I felt total happiness. It was a liberating, gentle, sweet sensation of...home. There was a beautiful statue of Brother Francesco across from me: he was sitting in a cross-legged position, looking out at the same valley I was looking at, smiling serenely. I chatted with him as I snacked, sang, wrote, and breathed deeply the air of Assisi.

And then, as seems to happen often there, the sky opened up, and it began to pour. Almost every day, the clouds would move over the landscape, dumping buckets of rain before they would, just as quickly, move on. I had brought a light raincoat and a small umbrella, both of which failed me quickly. I started to laugh, and I could feel both my dad and Brother Francesco laughing with me! We sang and laughed and teased the rain as I became completely drenched! It is a sweet memory of absolute blissful happiness.

Another memory is from when I went to see the Basilica of Saint Francis. It is a large, ornate church, pretty much everything that Brother Francesco didn't like and didn't want for himself. And yet, there it is. I wanted to walk through it, see the artwork, and – most of all – sit in the tomb where his ashes were, along with some of his Brothers' (especially Bernardo, Jacoba – the only female "brother" – and Leo, my soul twin). So, I was willing to breathe through the discomfort around all the fuss that I know he never would have approved of in order to have my own Holy Moment.

Entering the Basilica proved tricky, though, because I couldn't find the door! As I stood in the courtyard with my map and tour guidebook, I must have looked pretty pathetic. I made eye contact with a Brother, a man in the familiar brown sackcloth tied with a rope around the waist. He smiled, I smiled, and I approached him, using my Italian translation book to try to ask where the door was. He said, in English, "It's alright, I'm from Wisconsin. I'm Father Knowle." We chatted for a few moments about how he found his way there and the sacred service he provides as a tour guide. He also shared some fascinating historical trivia about the Basilica. He asked what brought me to Assisi, and, as often happened on that sabbatical, I started to cry as I explained what had called me there, showing him a book that I had prepared especially for this journey. He smiled and said, "Oh, you are a pilgrim." He immediately knew me in a way I could never explain. He knew I wasn't a tourist. He knew I was there because I was called there. And then, with the most gentle voice and caring heart, he asked, "May I pray over and anoint you before you enter the Basilica?" Through tears, I nodded that he could. He placed his hands on my head and spoke kind and gentle words that connected to my soul. It transformed this enormous and un-Francesco-like building into a most intimate encounter with the legacy that Francesco had left behind him.

I carried this Brother's blessing with me as I made my way through the Basilica to the tomb where Brother Francesco's ashes are kept. This was one of those moments in my life when I felt completely whole. No hum, no doubts, no misunderstanding that there was a reason for me. And I was living it.

A third sacred encounter happened at Eremo delle Carceri, a mountaintop retreat that the Brothers used to go to for quiet reflection time, away from the "city." After walking what seemed to be an endless road of switchbacks (which didn't exist back in Brother Francesco's time), I reached the top (and, there, I realized that I could have taken a cab!). Walking that climb meant the world to me. Along with the journey of depression – maybe hand in hand with it – I walk and live with an autoimmune disorder that causes intense pain throughout my whole body. For so many reasons, I *had* to make that walk. I absolutely needed to hike those steps myself, pain and all, if for no other reason than to prove to myself that I could do it.

Walking through the lush green woods of Eremo delle Carceri, I experienced again that feeling of being home, of feeling whole, of remembering my true self, spiritually, emotionally, humanly. I felt like I was the person I always saw myself as: connected to something larger than myself, a deeply loved child of God (God as Oneness, Wholeness, Spirit, Universal Love).

When I reached the cave where Brother Francesco would stay, again tears of gratitude poured from my eyes. This is the actual place where he faced his doubts, where he cried, where he refilled his well, where he would sing with the rain and talk with the birds, where he and God met in the most intimate of ways.

Before entering the cave, I sat in an adjoining room to prepare myself. As I was sitting in this sweet space, a woman walked past me to enter the cave. We nodded and smiled at each other, recognizing a fellow pilgrim (and not just another tourist mindlessly walking through). I was writing and reflecting on what had taken place on my journey to get to this place, what it meant for me as I moved forward in my life.

The woman came back out of the cave and stopped in front of me. She was slim, blonde, maybe my age or a little older. She was radiant. She bent down to me, put her hand on my arm, and whispered to me, *"Écouter"* (French for "Listen"). She smiled at me, truly knowing that we both deeply understood what she meant. And then, she left. And she was gone. I didn't see where she went, and there was just a single path out from the cave.

After a deep breath, I entered the cave.

As I am always drawn to do, I placed my hands on the stone wall of the cave and was overwhelmed with emotion (and "good bumps") as I heard music fill the space. There was no actual music playing – it was in my head, in my memory. It was the sound of my friend Suz playing a familiar song that we would sing on Sundays. And then, that song faded and what replaced it was my voice, singing and playing a song on the piano that I wrote for this Assisi journey. It was so clear. And then came a clear vision of Brother Francesco, smiling, standing with me, sharing this moment. I truly didn't want to move.

I was told to *Écouter.* I did. And I was given the most sacred of gifts.

I include these stories because I cherish the moments when the hum can't be heard. It's important for me to lift up the times when the darkness is obliterated by real light. I want to share these stories because, like so many, I truly lean into moments like these. Especially during the times when the darkness returns. They remind me that I – that all of us – can feel happy, connected, "normal," and, dare I say, blissed-out with life. We truly can.

And to always remember to *Écouter*.

I will, forever, remember to Listen.

Where Love Leads, Part One: From ASL to AK

When I was around thirteen, I was taken to a local theatre company, Fairmount Theatre of the Deaf, to see their production of an original play, *The Law of Silence*. This evening of theatre changed my life.

I fell in love with the story of this play, a beautiful historical drama about when monks used to rescue and teach sign language to deaf children, back in the days when deaf people would be slaughtered for being "defective." I fell in love with the actors in the play. I fell in love with sign language.

Already being immersed in the world of theatre as an actor and already feeling socially isolated most of the time, this new way of expressing myself felt absolutely perfect to me. And being around professional actors, adults doing something that I thought I might possibly want to do, was heaven.

I was the kind of child/teen/young adult who fell passionately and totally in love with many things.

I began learning Signed English (an older, archaic form of ASL, American Sign Language). I began to volunteer with the theatre company, ascending at one point to being a stage manager for a show. (I was very much in love with an actor in it, of course!)

I stuck around with this theatre company for almost four years before life, and other issues, distracted me.

Thirteen years later, after the hospital, after being told that I would never work or live on my own (and when I was doing both of those things, and more), The Universe led me back to this theatre company.

It was challenging. It tested my memory, my physical capabilities, my communication skills, my isolationist style of living, and my confidence.

I could not tell you how I did it. This was the beginning of a new spiritual journey for me. A new way of trusting in something, an Essence, larger than myself. Not the childhood "man-in-the-sky" God. This was something much more intimate than that. Much more powerful. I would come to understand it on a deeper level over the next two decades of my life.

Meanwhile, this new career path provided me the opportunity to work as an actor, teacher, interpreter, script translator, assistant to the artistic director, office manager, and whatever else needed to be done (which was just about anything and everything).

Love kept me working there for eight years. And then, Love led me to Alaska.

Where Love Leads, Part Two: Alaska

Before I reconnected with the theatre company of my teenage years, back in 1992, I was feeling lost and miserable, again.

I was working in a law office as an administrative assistant (although I had a much more accurate and much less attractive name for what I was doing!) and performing in really high-quality community theatre (the kind that I was truly proud of). I lived in an apartment I loved and couldn't afford. And I was in love with someone who, of course, had no intention of sticking around.

Life was feeling very...unhopeful. It seemed like the perfect time to try something a little radical.

I came across an opportunity to create an astrocartography chart for my life. The offer was simple: send my birth date, birth time, and three places I would like to live to this company (along with a minimal payment), and they would do an assessment of which place was best for me. It was not going to be a "you should live here" kind of result; it was more of a "this is what will unfold if you live here" concept. I figured, what the heck!

I chose my three locations for very specific reasons:

1. New York City. It had only been a few years since I had been kicked out of NYC after the whole hospital experience. I knew that I could never live there again, so I included it as a "ringer." If the company said it was a good place for me to live, I'd know that I'd wasted my money!

2. Missoula, Montana. I had a real passion for Montana (never having been there!)...the whole Big Sky idea and all. I had also filled out an application to the university there, on a whim, and never sent it. So, I thought, that would be where school would happen.

3. Anchorage, Alaska. Even though I had never been there, it always felt like my heart's home. There was some kind of strange pull to Alaska. If this process confirmed it, then there was something to this pull I felt.

When the envelope from the astrocartography people arrived, things were so dismal that I figured the results didn't matter, because I wasn't going anywhere. I just tossed it, unopened, into a box and forgot about it.

Much to my surprise, though, within a year, my entire life changed. I returned to work with what was then known as the Fairmount Theatre of the Deaf, and started traveling all over the country, having adventures, and developing many new skills, including becoming an American Sign Language interpreter.

Eight years later, after my life had completely transformed and I was working as a professional interpreter, I was unpacking my belongings in my new home in Anchorage, Alaska. I found the still-sealed astrocartography envelope and decided that it was probably time I opened it!

Here were the results, in a nutshell:

1. NYC. This place is toxic to your soul.
   Whew! Confirmation!

2. Missoula. A great place to go to school.
   Another confirmation!

3. Anchorage. Alaska is your soul's home.
   Bingo!

In addition to this, under the category of possible professions, it said interpreter. Really. It did.

After a month in Anchorage, I attended a past-life workshop where, among many other activities, there were astrological chart readings being done. The woman doing them thoroughly enjoyed my smile when she informed me that Alaska had been a place my soul had lived many times and that this was a true homecoming for me. Along with all of that, there was a small town that I had recently visited and fell in love with, Talkeetna. I had felt an immediate kinship with that place. Without telling her this, she shared with me that that land – specifically Talkeetna – was "my home" from a long time ago.

As my life unfolded so beautifully in Alaska, other aspects of what the astrocartography document predicted also came true: becoming a spiritual counselor was one of those predictions.

In Alaska, I felt like I could finally become my True Self. Like Michelangelo's *David* releasing himself from the block of damaged marble, I was being released from my old stories to live my life in a whole new and magnificent way, in a most magnificent place.

Spiritual Path

One of the main tools in my toolbox has been my connection with Spirit (God, Divine, Universe, the Big Kahuna, Love, whatever name works best for describing The Essence that is larger than we are). When I was young, it was God, a man in the sky who made decisions for us and who I relied on to take care of me. That image changed a bit when my dad died. Then, God became a punisher, my enemy, the thing that was trying to destroy my life.

I never stopped believing that there *was* a God. I just wasn't sure about what Its motives were.

As I learned and grew, as I explored different spiritual paths and beliefs and books, I found my way to a new relationship with this Energy that I can now call by any name. I understand It as an "It," an Essence, an always Creative, impersonal, and neutral Law of The Universe that we can use to change our lives and ourselves. (The rest of that story is already written in a whole lot of other books by other folks!)

Even as a young girl, though, sitting in our Reform Jewish

synagogue, I felt that God was bigger than any one single path.

It was in Anchorage that I discovered Ernest Holmes and the New Thought path of Science of Mind. A combination of philosophy, world religions, spirituality, scientific method, quantum physics, prayer, and love. I was amazed to discover that the life-long sense of God being both bigger than and also within me was not a new concept! It was a way of life. A way of being, learning, sharing, and connecting.

I also became aware of how this new spiritual path could potentially change the way I live with depression.

Immediately upon discovering the Spiritual Center in Anchorage, I knew I had found a home. The music, the method of praying, the language being used, the teachings being shared, it was all exactly what I had been searching for: God, both personal and infinite.

I dove, head-first, into service at the Center.

The Spiritual Center offered so many opportunities to serve, and I took every opportunity that I could! It connected deeply to the walk of all of my role models.

Most especially, Brother Francesco (known as Saint Francis of Assisi).

I served as greeter, sign language interpreter, musician and sub music director, speaker, board member, teacher assistant, teacher, workshop leader/creator, and supporter of all our different rituals and events. I loved being of service. It got me out of my own spirals and downward slides. It gave me purpose.

Also, I began taking classes. Learning the tools, mechanics, and history of this new-to-me form of spirituality. These classes were more than just book-learning, though. They offered me a mirror of who I had been, who I had been told I was, and who I wanted to become.

After completing the basic levels, I stepped into the more advanced classes, leading me to become a licensed spiritual counselor. It was during this training that I was able to release my attachment to medication for depression.

For me, the meds had never really helped. They masked my experience a bit, caused horrific side effects, and, in the end, never stopped the darkness from moving in. I tried many different brands and dosages and was left feeling tired, sick, and discouraged.

Throughout the spiritual counselor curriculum, I kept remembering The Summit, the moment with God and my dad when I decided to live. I decided – with the support of a wonderful therapist – that that conversation truly was enough for me. Depression or not, darkness or not, I was never going to end my life. I had promised.

So, the meds stopped.

After serving as a spiritual counselor for several years at the Center, offering prayer support and private sessions to those in our community and beyond, somewhat miraculously (although, it really was no miracle!), I transitioned into that now-well-known role of "wounded healer." Because of where I had been, I felt deep compassion for those who were still walking that path, just a little farther behind me.

I was feeling a very strong call to ministry and, at age forty-four, I was divinely guided to One Spirit Interfaith Seminary. I had finally found the place for me to grow, learn, and become a minister.

Through seminary, I learned about many of the world's religions and about ritual, ceremony, counseling, and generally how to be a minister in the world. Everything about it felt very much like how I wanted it to feel: simple, loving, open, and in alignment with all of my "soul team" guides. Although the program felt brief, in the grand scheme of my life, it had an immense and lasting impact on me. The teachers I learned from – and with – as well as the other spiritual seekers on the path with me in all of my classes and ongoing education have become yet another "family" for me.

After years of serving at my Spiritual Center, and then serving and speaking at Centers in different states, I heard loud and clear the call for the next step: a Center to call my own.

Inspired by Brother Francesco – and his beloved "Little Church" of San Damiano in Assisi, Italy - I wanted to create a space for spiritual exploration, learning, sharing, release, support, and family. I wanted to be of service on a whole new and deeper level.

In February of 2013, that dream became real: SpiritStone Spiritual Center was birthed into the world!

With the generous support of the community and the practical mind of my business partner, we were able to open the doors of this sweet, simple, spiritual community. Our mission was clear and easy to grasp: Everyone is Welcome Here!

We rented a lecture hall at the local university, and each Sunday, like a circus performer, I would arrive a couple hours before service time, rolling a suitcase and carrying bags filled with sacred items (and stones). Once in the room, the bags would be opened and the lecture hall would transform into a place of holiness: pashminas and throws, altar items that carried deep meaning, photos, totems...all kinds of goodies would make the place into our "little church."

Our gatherings were very low-key (some folks, including me, called us "the pajama church"). Folks would arrive, greeted by me at the door (this was super important to me; I don't care for the whole "hide-in-the-office-until-showtime" minister game), and they would choose a stone from the welcome table. We had a collection of handpicked river stones from many different places. They were beautiful and fascinating, and each one had a story. After choosing their stone (or having the stone choose them), attendants would sit down. The purpose of the stone was to hold it and infuse it throughout the service with whatever the person was carrying that they didn't want to carry anymore, whatever burden was on their heart. They could use it as a "worry stone" during the service until after prayer time when they were given an opportunity to release it (more to come on that in a moment).

We would sing a couple of welcoming songs together, which I got to play live on a really nice piano. There would be an announcement or two, a reading that related to the topic of the day, and then I would speak. I used PowerPoint slides, images, quotes, movie stories, personal stories, things I had learned, and simple observations to connect – I hoped – with where people were in their lives.

Preparing for the Sunday talks - and those wonderous PowerPoints - challenged the old story I had been told about depression, about how I would be living my life. The organizational thinking and clarity required to design each Sunday Gathering was sometimes difficult, true. It was always fulfilling, though.

Speaking spiritually, this is because I was never truly alone in the writing of the talk, the choosing of the slides, the discovery of the Sacred Reading and the songs we would sing. I was an instrument, a channel, of Something Larger than me. And that Thing didn't know anything about depression. Only that I was the one It was working through. And I was enough.

Back to the Gathering: After the talk, there would be a time of prayer, an affirmative kind of prayer (one that didn't beg or beseech a man-in-the-sky to "please, have mercy on us"), which would claim for us the Good that was ours and acknowledge that our struggles were always leading us to something better. And then, after the prayer, everyone was invited to bring their stone down to the front of the room where there was a blue crystal container filled with saltwater. Whatever they had infused into the stone could now be released; they didn't have to hold or carry it anymore. I would take those stones home, pray over them for several days, and then cleanse them to be ready to serve again.

Then, we'd give everyone an opportunity to support us, passing a small corduroy bag around so that no one could see what anyone else had put in it (because, to me, giving is not for show; it's a private thing for each of us). Finally, we'd have a closing blessing and song, and off everyone would go for the rest of their day. One hour, beginning to end!

And, like when the circus leaves town, I would pack up all of the pashminas and sacred items, collect the stones, and roll the bags back to my car, leaving behind no trace of our being there...except for the loving energy we created in that room together.

SpiritStone also provided opportunities for New Year's vision boarding (intentional collage), a labyrinth walk, movie-watching and discussion (and oh, the movies I chose!), and my favorite event: our All Saints gatherings. People would bring photos or tokens representing those who were no longer living, and we would create a beautiful altar for these precious remembrances. The service was filled with music, poetry, and story-sharing where people were given the opportunity to speak the names of those they were missing, share a story about what that person meant to them, cry and laugh and remember.

The All Saints Day ritual, particularly, gave me an opportunity to learn how to be vulnerable in front of "my flock." Especially after the deaths of Jimmy and Carl. Receiving permission from the community – and also giving myself that permission – to be Real, not just the figurehead of "minister," was a truly significant shift for me. That ritual will always remain for me a most cherished time with our community.

Once again, however, Object Permanence reared its familiar head, and things changed. What I thought would be my path for a much longer time came to a close. Due to circumstances not entirely in my control, I had to make a very difficult decision. I was moving, again. This time, across the country.

I chose to leave Anchorage in 2015, which meant closing the doors to that incarnation of SpiritStone, not knowing what would become of it in the future. This was quite possibly the most difficult part of leaving Alaska. I learned just how much impact our "little church" had had on folks and how much it meant to them.

The essence of our community continues – with a new name, SpiritsHome – and the work I do as a minister is mostly done virtually: via a website, on Facebook, through videos and postings, it is still in the world. And I hope, someday soon, Spirit will guide me to know what is to come next for this sweet, simple, spiritual Vision.

Camino Sagrado

Maddie and I prepared to leave Anchorage like two professional travelers getting ready for a life-changing journey. And it was!

Once again, I defied every prognosis and projection for what kind of person I would be and what kind of life I would live. Once again, I knew that I was not doing anything on my own. The Presence of that Essence-of-Many-Names was always with, around, in, and working through me to get everything needed done, done.

Having moved to Alaska with every single thing I had ever owned in my entire life (yes, I did that. It cost a small fortune), it was time to start letting things go. I released over one-thousand pounds of my belongings: a bookcase I loved dearly that I simply could not move one more time, a chair, clothes, DVDs, CDs, books (so many books), just so much stuff.

My car was small so we would be traveling light, Maddie riding shotgun. Only a small amount could be solidly packed in the car. A few boxes of books were sent on ahead through the postal service. The rest, I packed up and placed into the care of the moving company.

The decision to move out of Alaska was not an easy one. It was a process of "pros-and-cons" lists, support, counseling, weighing of options, and – ultimately – an admission of acceptance: The Universe had led me to Alaska where my life expanded. The Universe was now leading me somewhere else to do that again. I needed to trust.

We named our journey: Camino Sagrado (Sacred Path). Alaska to Ithaca, NY. By the end of this journey, I would be able to say I had been to all fifty states.

Friends hosted a lovely farewell gathering with lots of laughter, sharing, hugs, and – of course – food!

The morning we left a dear friend came to escort us to the highway entrance. It felt like when the munchkins dance Dorothy to the edge of Munchkinland in *The Wizard of Oz*.

Those first few days were the most concerning. I had asked several friends to travel the Alaska Highway portion with me because it is the most remote (fewer fuel stations, motels, etc). Each one wanted to and was unable to join me. The Universe was telling me, loud and clear, that I was not traveling alone. I needed to trust. Again.

We (me, Maddie, and God) traveled well. Long days of driving and then evenings in motels with our maps out and whatever was available on the local television station.

Our route was:

Anchorage to Tok (the last town in Alaska before crossing into Canada)

Tok to Teslin (Yukon Territory, Canada)

Teslin to Fort Nelson (British Columbia, Canada)

Fort Nelson to Whitecourt (Alberta, Canada)

Whitecourt to Great Falls (Montana)

Great Falls to Hulett (Wyoming)

Hulett to Thornton (Colorado)

Thornton to Des Moines (Iowa)

Des Moines to South Bend (Indiana)

South Bend to Cleveland (Ohio)

Cleveland to Ithaca (New York)

We would be up by 4:30 am and on the road by 6:30 am, driving until 5pm (most days).

The essential stops I wanted to make were in Wyoming (to see Devil's Tower), Colorado (to visit my sister), and Iowa (to visit The Field of Dreams). The rest of the adventure was open-ended. We wanted to be in Cleveland to celebrate Rosh Hashanah with my mom; that was our only time-oriented goal.

We saw the roaming bison herd in the Yukon (I have encountered them a time or two, this being my sixth time on the Alaska Highway). Maddie met some prairie dogs in Wyoming. We encountered the kindest dad in the world at a random fuel station who graciously removed the bird from my front grill (I didn't even see it hit us). We made friends during construction stops. We were generously upgraded to a suite at the motel in Great Falls. We were guided to the hotel in Indiana by the kindest of front desk clerks. We survived a scary night in Des Moines. We witnessed the difference in our country from the open skies and empty roads of Montana and Nebraska to the stress-filled and claustrophobic highways in Chicago.

And we made it to Ithaca. We arrived inspired, broken, open, and hopeful.

The first thing I put on our refrigerator door was the

poem *Ithaka* by Constantine P. Cavafy, which ends with these prophetic words:

Ithaka gave you the marvelous journey.
Without her you wouldn't have set out.
She has nothing left to give you now.

And if you find her poor, Ithaka won't have fooled you.
Wise as you will have become, so full of experience,
you'll have understood by then what these Ithakas mean.

When Things Make Sense

There are moments when I feel like – or what I imagine it must feel like to be – a normal person. Moments of happiness, wonder, bliss.

I almost included gratitude on that list, except that these days, even while living with and challenged by depression, I continue to feel gratitude. Even in the deepest, darkest moments, when tears are flowing, I can lie on my bed and scream my gratitude list out with fervent passion.

When I was in Italy – actually, when I was even just

planning for the journey to Assisi – I was filled with happiness and purpose. There was a sense of "the return," knowing that I was going to be walking in the footsteps of my soul's role model, Brother Francesco (St. Francis of Assisi). I had genuine fear about all of the unknowns, and yet I had the sense it was normal fear, not debilitating.

Sitting in the presence of the *David*, resting on the grounds of San Damiano, walking the endless trail of switchbacks up to Eremo delle Carceri where Francesco had prayed, seeing Sister Clare's hair and Francesco's robe...I felt happy. Simply happy. And I was filled with a holy wonder. A deep sense of wonder.

I've experienced many simpler, less dramatic moments of happiness as well. Like snuggling Maddie or walking with her around the block and feeling strong and good. Or moments of laughter that aren't burdened with any other complications.

In Assisi, after I got soaked by the sudden rain shower, I walked up the steep path to my room at Sacro Cuore to seek warm, dry clothes. As I did, I sang – loudly, like Brother Francesco would – and laughed, and felt completely free, weightless, unshackled from the darkness that held me down at other times of my life. Filled with the magnificent wonder that he must have felt when he sang with the rain.

As I walked through Eremo delle Carceri, tired and sore from the long hike to get there, I was filled with such wonder and awe. This is where he came for retreat, where all of the Brothers stayed...where they prayed, where he sang and cried, where they gathered to grow and go deep. There was absolutely no part of "depressed me" that existed in that place and at that time.

There are precious few of these moments, when things seem to make sense, when I feel like I am supposed to be here, when I remember that I am here on purpose, when the darkness is completely dispersed and there is only a sweet, comforting light surrounding me and shining within me. I hold onto moments like these with all of my strength.

The Pendulum

Picture a grandfather clock. Tall, stately, with a swinging pendulum inside the glass door. The pendulum swings consistently, calmly, without emotion or opinion. We pull the chains to wind the clock, and the pendulum responds. Always.

I have come to notice my emotional life can be like a pendulum. It gets wound up by life, circumstances, situations, encounters. And it responds to all of those. Except for one difference.

I have a choice as to how I interact with this pendulum.

I can witness the swings, or I can end up riding the pendulum, clutching for dear life to the movement of it.

When I choose to witness the swinging, I can see through the illusions. I can yield to frustrations and the illusion of roadblocks. I can lean into my Spiritual Practices and remember what is True. I can accept what I need to do and then do it. I trust. I allow. Everything becomes easier.

When I choose to ride the pendulum, life becomes a chaotic mess. It makes me the victim of failed systems, arbitrary (according to me!) rules, and fiery hoops that I feel forced to jump through. It is painful. I resist. Everything is "dumb." Life is "hard."

What is worse is that I am – my mind is – in charge of the choice I make. Yeah, that whole personal accountability piece. It always comes down to that.

Living with depression becomes something of a dance with the pendulum. A continual dance of negotiation. A perpetual dance of trust. An undeniable dance of choice.

The advantages of riding the pendulum are tempting: victimhood, release of responsibility, surrender (in the worst use of that word) to the big bad world, an excuse that gets me out of living my life. None of this carries any judgment. On the contrary, it is like that story of falling down the hole in the street. It's "not my fault." At least, that's how it feels – and how I interpret it – when I am riding the pendulum.

It takes strength to witness the swinging. The ability to get up and move, to acknowledge accountability, to take the steps needed to do what needs done, to look all of the excuses right in their face and say, "So what?!?" Being able to do this does not make me – or anyone – a better person. Sometimes it simply means making use of that well-known phrase: I am "faking it until I make it."
It is not a one-or-another kind of deal. Yesterday, I witnessed the pendulum and felt really good about how

things were going. This morning, I woke up clinging to the already swinging pendulum and felt like there were no other options.

Learning how to let go of the pendulum - mid-swing - and remember that I will land safely, on my feet, where I can shake myself off and begin witnessing again, well, that is a life-long process. A process that requires - for me - trust, prayer, and the scariest of all qualities, vulnerability.

To be vulnerable enough to say, "It is scary to let go. I feel afraid that I might not be strong enough. What if nothing changes when I let go? What if I am simply not able to witness again, like I have done before? What if holding on tight to the pendulum is the way I will live from now on?"

And then, to be even more vulnerable in listening for the answers:
> It can feel that way.
> You are.
> It will.
> You will be.
> It isn't. Let go.

So, I try. I take a deep breath. I listen. I pray. I ask. I open up. I become willing.

And I loosen my grip, slowly, finger by finger...

A Little Help

When I am walking Maddie during cold, snowy days, she refuses to wear dog booties. We have tried. She either shakes them off (and we lose them in the snow) or pretends that she absolutely cannot walk in them and wants them taken off immediately. So, we walk without them.

Being an Alaskan dog, she loves winter, she doesn't mind the cold, and she loves to dig her nose into the snow to smell whatever might have wandered through it before she got there.

Sometimes, though, she will get salt in between the pads on her paws (or tiny ice balls that freeze up in her foot fur). And, as we are walking along, she will start to limp a bit and then, eventually, she will stop and hold up her leg, the one with the frozen, salty paw. And she will wait. She will look at me as if to say, "A little help here, please."

And I will reach down and clear her paw of the ice ball or salt, and she will immediately recover and begin her happy trot once again. Crisis averted, pain over, memory of it released.

This got me thinking. I realized that much of my ongoing struggle comes from my not letting go of a painful moment that stopped or slowed me down.

The moment is in the past; the event – however painful and distracting – is not happening anymore. And yet, I am still limping from it. Or worse. I am still standing there with my figurative paw in the air, waiting for someone to clear out the salt and ice and detritus that has caused me to stop walking onward.

Here's the thing – and I know you know what's coming: no one is going to clear that up for me. There's no one else here except me to take care of it.

Well, that is not entirely true.

As a spiritual person, I know that I am not totally on my own. Ever. I know that through Spiritual Practice, there is a way to get my "paw" back to working order. When I do the work (the Spiritual Work, that is), I am more able to clear the frozen, salty memories that are preventing me from walking strong and tall in my present and on into my future.

In addition to Spiritual Practice, we can also get a little help from our friends, from those people we trust: family, clergy, therapist, doctor, and – as Maddie likes to remind me – our beloved furry companions. Although Maddie lacks the thumbs needed to clear out her own paws, she is quite skilled at reminding me how to be Grateful in the Present Moment and to remember that there is a whole lot of Good in my life.

So, two ideas came to me from this moment with Maddie. The first: There is no need to carry past pain around with us forever. Once it shows up for us (like salt in the paw), we can choose to do the work to find a way to clear it, heal it, release it, and walk onward.

The second idea is that it is okay to ask for a little help in dealing with whatever it is that has stopped us in our tracks.

I think we can all agree that everyone is carrying some kind of ice ball or salt inside themselves. We may not want to be carrying it. We may have thought we had taken care of it a long time ago, had resolved it and moved on, thinking we were all healed. And then, like a surprise that no one wants, the pain or discomfort returns.

When these moments arise, I do not always like to admit that it is happening. I want to show the world my "best self," to be the one who helps others and does not need any help for herself. So, I do not always choose to show the world my paw, the weakness or injury or pain I am feeling within me.

If this is true for me, the chances are good that it might be true for other people. We can't always know or see what kind of help is needed. It's not always as simple as Maddie lifting up her paw and looking at me with those eyes that are so clearly asking for assistance.

Well, here comes the cliché we have all heard: We all need a little help every now and then. The Beatles immortalized this truth with their song "With a Little Help from My Friends." Ram Dass shared the phrase, "We are all just walking each other home." We all know this to be true, that we sometimes need help and that others sometimes need it as well.

It all comes back to Kindness. I could ignore Maddie's raised paw, the plaintive look in her eyes, the stubborn immovable stance she chooses to take. I could simply say, "Pull it together, girl. Let's get moving." However, that would not be kind. And I would not want someone to say that to me.

Maddie continues to teach me how to be a better person, a better friend, and a better minister. This time, she taught me that we all need a little help every now and then. Help to relieve and release some pain that is keeping us from moving forward. Help that can give us all a boost to be able to continue trotting happily along the path of life.

Moments of My High Resolve

Keep fresh before me
the moments of my high resolve.
— *For the Inward Journey*, Howard Thurman

The moment I stood in front of the *David*.

The moment I survived Lava Falls.

The moment I forgave the man who raped me.

202

The moment I promised God and my dad that I would stay.

The moment I was ordained.

The moment I realized why I had become a minister.

The moment I passed Algebra 054.

The moment I sang "Superstar" for Jimmy.

The moment my mom and I told each other "I love you" and it was real.

The moment I walked to the cabin, in pain and afraid of bears, singing.

The moment I moved to Alaska.

The moment I left Alaska, for the last time.

The moment I stood in Francesco's cave.

The moment I blessed the ocean with people from all over the world.

The moment I passed Courage Training with Dan Millman.

The moment I recorded "Don't Let It Bother You" at Michael's apartment.
The moment Anita and I sang "Here" at Michael's memorial.

The moment musicians said "Yes" to a SpiritStone fundraiser concert.

The moment we opened the doors to SpiritStone.

The moment I recorded "inward fire" and "namaste."

The moment I returned to school after my dad died.

The moment I put aloe on Anita's radiation burns.

The moment I became my family's minister.

The moment I met Todd Rundgren and Utopia.

The moment I told Carl I loved him so he'd know.

The moment I climbed Mount Subasio.

The moment I became "Rev Rachel 4.0" to my mom.

And this moment. And this one. And this one.

What is important for me to remember is that before each of these moments, there were moments like the ones I so often struggle with. Before I could reach the moments of my high resolve, I had to climb out of the moments of my lowest depths.

And I did it. And I can do it again. I am doing it. Right now.

"I Am Still Learning"

Michelangelo once said, "I am still learning." This from the man who released his *David* from a block of damaged stone.

During my journey to Italy in 2009, I got to sit in the presence of *David*. The most powerful moment for me was the realization that Michelangelo brought that statue to life by listening, without any ego interference. His creation was not designed, planned, predicted. He didn't have a strategic plan set out for it. He didn't have notes or preliminary drawings. He had a damaged block of stone and had been told that nothing would come of it. And then he listened.

He talked about how he released *David* from the stone. He didn't chisel him or "make" him happen. It was more than that. As Michelangelo chiseled at the stone, *David* became aware of his own existence, and he guided Michelangelo to let him out. He was shown what to cut away, and it was everything that was *not David*.

This says so much to me about all of our lives. How do we get out of the way to allow our greatness to be brought out? How do I do that? We all have the capability, wisdom, passion, creativity, and desire to do something with our lives. If we aren't yet doing it, why aren't we? What's in the way?

I felt so inspired in that moment, sitting in front of *David*. And in the days and months after, I still felt inspired. And then, I experienced what Howard Thurman described as the grit and dust of daily life. That is what got in my way. That moment of my high resolve faded, and I went back to life as usual.

It's kind of like when we visit the chiropractor, and for a short time afterward we consciously sit up straight. And then, after a bit of time passes, we notice that we're slouching again, neck jutted out, hunched over. So we straighten back up and think, "I need to pay more attention!" And we think we've got it now. And then a short time passes and, surprise! Slouching. How does that happen? By not paying attention.

The thing is, is it even possible to pay *that much* attention? All the time?! While still being in the world? I mean, okay, if I were a monk on a mountain and my entire day consisted of drinking tea, writing, reading, and sitting up, I could probably master it. That's not my life, though. I have to contend each day with convincing myself to get out of bed, negotiating whether to brush AND floss or just brush, getting the dog taken care of, and then arguing with myself about how to be productive versus sitting on the couch with my phone.

Yep, I'm still learning.

Maddie

I made the decision to fill out the paperwork and complete the assessment for Maddie to become a licensed Emotional Support Animal (ESA). Yes, I know, we've all heard about the abuses of this title and of the debacle of the emotional support peacock being brought onto an airplane, as well as all of the other – dare I use the term – "crazy" ways people attempt to take advantage of this important resource. That is not to say that any animal could be passed over as *not* being emotionally supportive. I truly believe that all animals, as pets or seen in the wild, bring us a measure of comfort, an appreciation of life, even a sense of peace. There are deer in my neighborhood, and I always smile when I see them. They remind me to be aware that I am sharing their land with them.

However, as I often find myself searching for my next home, and occasionally I might travel, I thought it was time for me to make Maddie "official." There is no doubt that she has emotionally supported me. From the moment we met – at only eight weeks, she was already filled with personality – I knew that we would be companions. She has always been there for me, ready to provide comfort and humor and vitality to my life. In dark times, she is the reason I get out of bed and put on pants. On my best days, she is happy to snuggle with me or celebrate my feeling good by trotting along the sidewalk as we stroll around the block. She has kept me alive and I have been her safe place since I held her in my arms at just eight-weeks.

What was both shocking and somewhat hilarious was the process I had to go through to validate her getting licensed as an ESA. I thought *she* would have to go through some kind of training (which she would pass, of course!). No, it was quite the other way around! *I* had to go through the ringer for this! I had to answer a questionnaire that – frankly, by the end of it – had me thinking that I should be hospitalized immediately! As I reviewed my own answers, I thought, "Holy Handbags! I have survived A LOT! How have I done that?" It was both inspiring and a bit disturbing what I had shared. However, I wanted to be completely honest so that the folks evaluating us would realize how essential Maddie is to my life. Still....

Looking at my own history of living with depression, the experiences I have had, the struggles I have survived, the "adventures" and misadventures I have navigated, the challenges I have conquered....Well, let me just say, I didn't know whether I should be impressed or deeply concerned!

And, still, after all of that somewhat disheartening reflecting, when I completed the call with the licensing therapist and received the news that Maddie was definitely and officially approved as an ESA, I felt a sense of accomplishment. Maybe even a little bit of validation. The therapist was impressed with how I had learned to live, even before Maddie entered the picture. And she felt assured that Maddie is definitely an important part of my daily appreciation of living.

Most importantly, after answering those questions and documenting all of those stories, the saga of my life, here is what really matters: I am still here with Maddie by my side (snoring, at this moment).

We are here for each other (I am pretty sure that I am *her* ESA!). Grateful, always Grateful, for all that has happened to both of us, for everything that has brought us here, for all of the moments that we have already shared. And ready for the next adventure, the next moment. Together.

It Can Get Noisy

The noise in my head is sometimes louder than the noise outside of it.

There is a strange kind of noise that comes with depression.

Sometimes it's that hum I've written about, the fluorescent light hum. Sometimes it's a voice shouting cruel and untrue things. Sometimes it's the voice of those who are no longer here, encouraging me to hang on. Sometimes it's like traffic: loud, obnoxious, invasive. And sometimes it's a whisper. That creepy, scary movie kind of whisper. The one you don't ever want to hear. The one that makes you feel like there's no escape.

The noise can be happening while I'm in a conversation. Or working. Or walking the dog. Or writing (quite often when I'm writing). It can show up when someone is trying to tell me that it's going to be okay. Or when we're making plans to go do something.

The noise is different from The Knights. They are very specific voices with a clear and relentless agenda.

The noise is just...well, noise. Like in a David Lynch movie. Kind of industrial, kind of like a crowd scene in a movie, kind of like a cacophony of all different kinds of sounds. It makes meditation a very challenging practice. I mean, the whole point of meditation is to "quiet the mind." This noise is not very cooperative. I try to meditate, and the noise just gets louder. Attempts to quiet my mind are the equivalent of me standing in the middle of Times Square and yelling, "Could everyone just cool it for a minute? I mean, really people! Tone it down!"

It's difficult to explain. When someone is talking to me, and the noise is going strong, they think I'm not listening or that I'm spacing out or just not truly paying attention to them (which most people find rude). And I usually play it off that I was distracted by something acceptable: a thought, something I needed to remember to do, a homework assignment idea...

The noise is isolating.
The noise is incessant.
The noise is a problem.
The noise never goes away.

Me and Jacob

In the Hebrew Bible, one of my favorite stories is the one about Jacob wrestling with the angel.

"Jacob remained alone, and a man wrestled with him until daybreak. The man saw that he could not defeat Jacob, and he touched the joint of Jacob's thigh. Jacob's hip became dislocated from wrestling with him. And The man said, 'Let me go for dawn is breaking.' Jacob said, 'I will not release you unless you bless me.' The man said 'What is your name?' Jacob said, 'Jacob.' The man said, 'Your name shall no longer be called Jacob, rather Israel, for you have struggled with God and with man and you have been victorious.' Jacob asked, and said, 'Please tell me your name.' The man said, 'Why are you asking for my name?' And he blessed him there. And Jacob called the place Peniel [God's face], 'For I have seen God face to face and my soul was saved.' The sun rose as he left Peniel."

There are many scholarly theories and interpretations of this story, and they all have validity. My experience of the story is much more personal.

The way I experience it is that Jacob would not let go until he was renamed, transformed, seen as his true self (in spiritual terms: True Self).

I wrestle with God, my *human* self wrestles with God, as I am always fiercely trying to live more as my True Self, the one more connected to Spirit, the one that can rise out of and above the darkness, the one that doesn't get caught up in the dramas that we humans create for ourselves, the one that knows that depression does not define me or my life.

I wrestle with God. The darkness wrestles with the light. Sometimes, when people witness or sense that this wrestling is taking place, they think it looks like I am holding on to the darkness. Just like it probably looked like Jacob was holding on to the angel.

I'm wrestling with it.
I'm dancing with it.
I'm negotiating with it.
I'm seeking the blessing from it.

Until I remember, or learn, my new name. Until I am transformed and can see, on my own, my True Self.

The Deep End

When we are dealing with physical pain – chronic, tormenting, persistent – it can be difficult to function: to pay attention, to focus, to organize our thoughts. And if you're someone like me, who is also battling depression on a moment-to-moment basis, adding pain on top of that is kind of a nightmare scenario.

I was describing it to a friend the other day. The analogy came out like this: If I am dropped into the deep end of the pool, my first thought isn't the sudden desire to become a better swimmer. It is the desperate need to get the heck out of the deep end.

As a minister, I know how important and powerful prayer can be. It doesn't really matter what the prayer is or who it is directed to; the simple act of speaking affirming words of Truth can change how we experience a situation. Because that's what prayer does. It doesn't change "things," it changes *us*, how *we* feel, see, and live through a moment. So, I know that prayer works.

And...

When the pain is so intense that it scares me, that it

causes me to not be able to move, when it interferes with daily actions (like getting out of bed or brushing my teeth), even the most enthusiastic of prayers cannot move me. It feels like I am trying to learn how to be a better swimmer. All I want is some help getting to a place in the pool where I can put my feet down.

It is about finding a place of safety from the fear. A place of respite from the attack (or perceived attack). It is about finding Light from inside the darkness. Finding Truth from inside the illusion. Finding Courage to say, "This is not Real, not Reality as I Know it to be. This is not how God Sees me."

In the midst of the darkness, it is essential to remember how God Sees me: as someone who tries, who never gives up. Someone who can tolerate pain and still smile. Someone who can be struggling to get out of bed and still find a way to be Grateful.

It is not always easy to remember this. It is absolutely essential, though.

Because when we are thrown into the deep end, there is a panic that starts that doesn't help us save ourselves (or be helped, by the way). Flailing and splashing and gasping for air doesn't help us. However, trying to "get quiet" in the midst of a moment when we think we are drowning is not all that realistic an expectation either.

It seems to come down to Trust. Ah, that word. Trusting in what, though? Well, for me, it is trusting in what I Know is Truth: That Spirit has me, regardless of what it looks or feels like. Trusting that Good is always unfolding, even when I can't see it with my human eyes, feel it with my human senses, or brain. Trusting that — and here come the eye rolls from the cynics! — that there is something here for me to learn, an opportunity to grow, a moment of expansion for me that will, inevitably, transform me, and I will come away from each moment stronger.

I have to Trust these things. I have to. Otherwise, I wouldn't survive a single day on this planet.

And the moment I remember, to yield and allow myself to fully Trust, I can feel my feet touching the bottom of the pool. And I Know I am Safe.

When I am able to stand - or sit - in the place of Knowing, then I become able to also see the Truth for others. To see how God Sees them, Sees you, even if you can't see it yet yourself.

Regardless of "beliefs" or "dogma."

We *are* safe.

I *See* you.

Flying High

Don't be concerned about being disloyal to your pain
by being joyous.
~ Pir Vilayat Inayat Khan

Balancing moments of happiness, light, pure joy,
laughter, and release with the experience of depression
is a fascinating experience.

A couple of days ago was my birthday. If there's one
reason to be on Facebook, it's to have a birthday there.
Hundreds of expressions of love and appreciation and
gratitude for my being on the planet...there is nothing
quite like that, especially for someone who has become
something of a recluse. I mean, I certainly couldn't handle
being at a party or gathering with all of those people.
Receiving these missives of sweetness, one at a time,

from people I have met (and some I haven't met yet) during the many stages of my life, from different states, careers, schools, Spiritual Centers...it was spectacular.

So I was happy. Jubilant, even. Excited. Laughing. Smiling. I felt alive, lifted, and carried. I was feeling like I hadn't felt in a very long time.

And at the same time, there was this underlying voice saying, "Be careful." When I asked what that was about, what started to come through was this:

Don't fly too high; you might come across as bipolar. You don't want that.

I worked with a psychiatrist many years ago who insisted on misdiagnosing me as bipolar because I expressed anger at her. The fact that I "came out" of my depressive state to say I was angry caused her to impose upon me an entirely different – and inaccurate – diagnosis. She put this in my records, and it took years to have that label removed. The sting of that incident has stayed with me.

Don't fly too high; people might think you're "all better."

"You were laughing today, I saw you smiling," they might

say. "I'm so glad you're over it. So relieved you've gotten past that whole depression thing." How do I explain that this is just a moment of relief? How do I express my gratitude for feeling the lightness and laughter – understanding that it is a fleeting and beautiful moment of blessed relief – without sounding like I am attached to the depression or that I "want" it?

Don't fly too high; when the sadness – which never really left you – resurfaces, people won't believe you were really grateful for their kindness. Or, even worse, they'll be disgusted that this wasn't enough to heal you and get you moving on.

Imagine being very sick for a long time and then starting to recover. You make it from the bed to the couch, and then maybe one day you make it to the mailbox. Suddenly, everyone is excited that you're all better, and they think that the sickness is gone. If you show any lingering symptoms, it brings up some impatience. "Come on, you were doing so great. Don't stop fighting now, keep getting better."

Don't fly too high; the crash will hurt more than you can ever imagine.

In those amazing moments when the darkness lifts, my first thought – my first fear – is, "Oh God, does feeling good mean I am bipolar? Can I feel happiness, can I feel hope, can I laugh? Is this how normal people feel? Or does it mean I am having a manic episode? Is it just another diagnosis? Or is this what it feels like to not be in the depression?"

Next comes, "How long will this last? Is it only dependent on outside forces, or is this coming from within me? How can I be sure? How can I rely on it?"

And given time, it becomes, "What does this mean? Am I done? Can I sustain this or hold on to it? Will it last? Can I just let myself feel good?"

So, things start getting better. At least they – and I – start to feel better. The darkness seems to be lifting. What does that mean? Am I allowed to feel better? Is it safe?

Can I trust this?

And then the tears come, for no good reason, just after feeling really good, and many of those questions are answered.

Yes, it's safe to feel good when it happens.

No, it doesn't mean I am bipolar.

Yes, I can feel hopeful and happy. I can have my moments of high resolve.

No, I can't hold on to it, so I should enjoy it while it's happening.

Yes, it can happen because of outside reasons, and that's okay.

No, I am not done. I won't ever be done.

With depression, there really isn't any getting "over it," "getting past it," or even a solid experience of "getting better." There's just getting up each day and trying again. The questions that return to my mind again and again are: How do I balance moments of pure joy with this experience of living in the darkness? Is there a way to feel true happiness without feeling guilty about it? And when, if ever, will it be safe for me to simply feel each of my emotions – purely, genuinely – without the fear of the darkness returning?

As always, the only answer to all of these questions remains: I am still learning.

Love Returns

Enter The Red Knight.

After a long stretch of time believing that Love was not possible for me, getting used to the idea of being alone – well, with Maddie of course – and accepting this as my life's truth, Love returned. Wait, let me clarify what I mean by Love (with an intentional "big L").

This was not a romantic, Hallmark movie love. This was not something I "fell into." It was much deeper than that. It was a Love based on truly Seeing and Knowing another person, spiritually as well as humanly. Not physical. No violins, no hearts and flowers.

This was unexpected, surprising, not conventional. A moment to talk and listen and sit and be with someone in a whole new way. Honestly. Authentically. A "test drive" of my commitment to be fully present and to "mean what I say and say what I mean."

True Communication. Commitment to showing up in honesty, integrity, and Kindness.

The kind of Love I had always wanted. The kind that held much more meaning for me.

A few days of this kind of connection, this possibility, left me feeling like I'd never felt before: confident, excited, energized at the new way things were unfolding. Feeling safe in a way I had never experienced before.

And, right on cue, in it rode. Both Knights showed up, actually: The Knight of the Mirrors as well as The Red Knight. One arrived to break me, the other to show me the truth - as they see it - so that I will stop now, before it's too late.

The attack is always swift and merciless:

"How could you ever think this was possible? Have you forgotten already who you are? Have you lost your ability to understand that you're broken, unworthy, a fraud, a disaster, a failure? You belong with no one. You belong to us. You belong alone. You need to wake up."

And just like that, everything I felt, experienced, believed, from the past week was gone. It was all a lie. A trick of the light. Love didn't really return; it never will. Give up.

Except for this one problem: THIS ISN'T TRUE. It simply isn't the Truth.

Depression, however it chooses to show up, always lies. Yes, it protects me, it keeps me thinking I'm safe, it comforts me and gives me excuses not to show up (or leave the house).

And it lies. It's what fuels the Knights. Or they fuel it, maybe. That doesn't matter. All that matters is that I remember what's True and Real.

I'm grateful for all of my teachers: sadness, grief, the darkness, the Knights.

I've been a stellar student. I've earned a master's degree in survival.

"What's My Answer?"

A friend shared this story with me:

225

A woman was running from something that scared her. It was some kind of monster chasing her, running her down hard. She ran as fast as she could and never seemed to gain enough ground to get away. She took a quick turn, which led her down an alley and smack into a dead-end brick wall. The monster was right there, standing in front of her. She was trapped.

She knelt down and, in a shaky voice, asked: "What are you going to do with me?"

The monster calmly replied, "I don't know. It's your nightmare."

Recently, both Knights staged a relentless assault on me. The Red Knight and The Knight of the Mirrors both showed up strong, full force. I felt myself cowering in fear, begging for mercy, praying for relief, promising that I would never try to do anything again that would cause their rage or return.

I shared this moment with my friend, and she told me that story.

My first reaction was to defend the Knights, to validate their existence: "I'm not making them up! They're REAL!"

What was worse is that I actually believed - in some strange way - that I owned the right to have them, to keep them, to not allow them to become just another imaginary trauma I brought on myself.

I defended my right to be attacked.

When someone lives in the darkness, there is a certain amount of safety and security in that. There's a good deal of ownership. It doesn't come from a place of ego, more from a place of being afraid to want more, afraid to discover that I'm not deserving of more. Deserving of Love, of happiness, of a life that could be free of the Knights.

I cling to the Knights because, in some way, I understand they are taking care of me, keeping me from taking risks and getting hurt, keeping me from leaping and possibly falling.

When I realized that my friend understood this, when I felt heard and seen and understood, the Knights actually retreated. Backed away. I got my answer.

Unfair

Life's good
But not fair at all.
~ Lou Reed

Back in 1987, when I was in the depths of an episode of intense darkness in the psych unit in New York City, I pondered that the whole experience of depression was simply not fair.

I would attempt to explain to the doctors and nurses, to my friends and family, to anyone who would listen, that it felt like if I had cancer – or a more "visible" illness – more people would have a better, or more patient, more understanding of the battle I felt I was fighting. And I would have a more tangible demon to face.

I understood then – and understand now – how terrible that sounds. How selfish and even somewhat ridiculous it sounds to "wish" for a physical ailment rather than a mental/emotional one. However, the demons of the mind are quite formidable opponents. Most especially because they are not tangible.

Those demons that lurk, that hide, that speak only to us from within, those are the most frightening. No one else can see or hear them, and only a small few can fully understand what it is like to live with them: to be constantly saying, "Stop talking to me" or "Yes, I hear you" or some other response that feels like a negotiation, like a way to survive their attacks.

It can feel exhausting. And it can feel so very unfair. And yet, here we are, alive, in this life, on this earth at this very moment. We are interacting with others; we are in families and communities, in classrooms and workspaces, grocery stores and oil change places. We are here. We are essential pieces in The Cosmic Jigsaw Puzzle of The Universe. If we were not essential pieces, we would not be here. There are no accidents in Creation.

I had a moment of crying in my car, feeling sad, feeling alone, feeling lost. I pulled into the vehicle emissions testing site and went to sit on an uncomfortable folding chair to wait. I was totally in my own dark bubble of sad, when the gentleman next to me said, "Well, hello there! How were your holidays?" We then had a most lovely conversation about his eighty-nine years on the planet, his fifty-five years of marriage, his thirty years since retirement that he has used to plant gardens, and our appreciation for being alive and meeting one another. The moment before this one, I felt alone. Now, I felt energized. This man recharged my soul. He reminded me (Re-Minded me) that I am not alone and that we all have a reason for being here, even if it is just to share a moment with a stranger. To lift one another up.

We walk this tightrope of life, this balance beam of living. We feel scared, invigorated, sad, inspired, excluded, invited, alone, immersed, happy, worried, comforted, anxious, ready, and terrified...Alive. Always alive.

Is life fair? I used to say that "fair" was the other four-letter word starting with "f." Is it fair that some suffer while others do not? Or that some have more than they need while others scramble to simply get by? No, it is not fair.

Does that really matter, though? We are all here for a reason, whether we know it – or like it – or not. If we did not have a reason to be here, we would not be here. Again, there are no accidents in Creation.

So, when the demons get loud, when the pain intensifies, when I am feeling like I just do not understand anything, when the darkness moves in, what can I do – what can we do – to get through it?

We can remember:

The voices are not real.
The tightrope is safe.
We are not alone (even when we think we are).
There is a reason we are here.
Pay attention.

Let's stop worrying about what is fair or not fair and just be here. In our sadness and in our darkness and in our pain and in our challenges. Let's just be here. Right now. With ourselves. With each other. For ourselves and for each other.

A Second Chance

My introduction to Dan Millman was in 1988, as I was recovering from the hospital experience in New York. I read *Way of the Peaceful Warrior,* and my life began to change.

In 1996, I got to meet Dan when he was in Cleveland doing an evening talk and book signing. At that point, I had just finished his book *No Ordinary Moments,* and I knew that this man was going to be one of the most influential teachers I would ever encounter.

In 2003, I went to San Rafael, California, for a week-long Courage Training with Dan and his three team teachers. There were about twenty-four people like me in the room, ranging in age from seventeen to sixty-something, and from all over the world. We bonded immediately, becoming a supportive tribe of seekers, people focused on becoming stronger, wanting to heal whatever in us felt broken.

We exercised our bodies (doing the Peaceful Warrior workout). We exercised our minds as we learned new ways of thinking and looking at ourselves and our lives. We ate healthy meals together. And we learned how to knife fight (using little pieces of rubber tubing as our weapons).

The metaphor was that learning how to handle ourselves in a knife fight would help us face whatever else was coming at us in the world, be it from co-workers, strangers, loved ones, family, whatever. The strategy one uses in a knife fight, which is more about how we *think* about what's happening and how to handle it, is a strategy that we can use in our daily lives.

We all laughed when Dan joked that Tai Chi is wonderful, except it's only effective if you're being attacked in slow motion. (He was, indeed, joking. He completely understands the value of Tai Chi!)

We watched films with elaborate and exciting sword fights – most notably *The Princess Bride*. And we practiced with each other, learning how to step in when it was time to step in and to step aside when it was time to step aside.

He said that it is important to stand in our truth. However, if we're standing in our truth on train tracks and a train is coming right at us, it might be wise to adjust our truth a few inches to the side.

The final "test" was a knife fight scenario (with our little rubber knife, of course), being confronted by all three of Dan's team teachers as he and the whole group watched. After all those days together, there was so much love and support in the room, it felt like we all could do anything. Once we passed the test, we would get a certificate and be celebrated by everyone in the room.

Three people didn't pass, including me. I knew what I needed to do, I was prepared, my practice partner was cheering me on, everyone was encouraging. I just couldn't do it. I was fearful. I was stuck in my head trying to "think" my way out of it. Dan saw this and kept encouraging me, reminding me that my over-thinking wasn't serving me. I couldn't hear him. I kept backing away. I couldn't get myself to step into into the fight as I had been taught to do. I was so ashamed of myself.

After everyone had gone, Dan looked at the three of us who hadn't passed and said, "Would you like a second chance?"

Hearing those words, something broke loose within me. I started crying. The tears were coming from a very deep place, a place that always only ever wanted a second chance, at anything. A second chance to say goodbye to my dad. A second chance to do things differently in high school. A second chance to make amends for how I abused my body for so many years. A second chance with anyone I ever loved who left. So many second chances that I always wanted and never got.

We all took that second chance. And we all passed the test.

During that second time, as I faced the three "attackers,"

one of them looked me right in the eyes and said, "Rachel. Go straight to the heart of danger, and there you will find safety."

I let go of everyone in that room, everything around me, every story I had ever told myself, every story I had ever heard about myself, everything I ever believed about myself that wasn't true...and I stepped in.
A second chance allowed me to become courageous.

Second chances – in every aspect of life – have become something I cherish. Something I am always willing to give. And something I am always Grateful to be given.

Falling and Rising

There have been times when I have taken risks, thinking that the risk might lead to happiness. Those risks were mostly around falling in love with someone, taking the chance to give my heart without wondering if it's the "wisest decision."

Some people in my life have responded to this in a way I'd describe as discouraging – a wet-blanket approach of "Are you sure they feel the same?" or "Here we go again, same old story." I know their responses reflect their fear that I'll get hurt. They seem to forget that getting hurt is easy for me. Seeking happiness takes real courage.

It's like falling down and getting back up.

Falling down is easy, effortless; we don't have to do anything, because gravity takes care of everything for us. We just fall. In fact, falling down often happens without our permission; it happens out of our control.

Now, the getting up part, that is the real work. There might be embarrassment or humiliation attached to the fall. Rising from the fall takes courage and strength to face the fears of mockery or the pain caused by the fall, or even the fear of falling again.

I will always take the risk. It is always worth it.

And, as long as I do that, I will continue to find the courage to rise again.

Who Am I?

Am I this broken, unlovable thing that I think I am in my darkest moments?

Am I this triumphant, strong, courageous person that I think I am in my brightest moments?

Am I the role model for recovery that some see me as? Am I a farce, a fake, a liar because I still struggle through this pain?

Am I Reverend Rachel, the one who understands and feels compassion and can help, encourage, and support others?

Am I little rachel who still feels abandoned, forgotten, not chosen, left behind, never to be loved?

Am I the healthy, no-meds, forging-through-depression warrior?

Am I the weak, can't-stop-crying, isolating, fragile one?

Am I the spiritual seeker?

Am I the great avoider of all things earthly?

Can I be all of those people and still survive? How?

Most of the time, I know I am a:

woke-up-Grateful, doing-her-best, Dorothy-on-the-yellow-brick-road, moth-struggling-to-emerge, just-trying-to-love, storytelling, Maddie-snuggling, bacon-eating, song-writing, humor-finding, honesty-attempting, still-breathing human being.

Who are you? Be gentle when you answer this, please. Forgive the parts of you that are not what completely or perfectly you'd like to be. And, find the Truth of the Real you.

Strong. Resilient. Broken. Trying...Every day.

The Constant

In algebra, there are variables (x, y, etc.) and there are constants (...ummm, I guess those are numbers...I really don't understand algebra!).

Love has been the one thing that always comes to my rescue.

When I remember this, I return to life, to my True Self.

Love Awakens me.

Love never leaves me.

Love is my constant.

Word of the Year

A few years ago, inspired by an idea from my mom, I added a new ritual to my New Year's Eve tradition. Along with watching *The Poseidon Adventure* (in memory of my soul twin, Jimmy), eating something that is considered "naughty" (this year it's rye bread with salmon cream cheese), and creating a Vision Board, I added the ritual of choosing a word and a mantra to guide and inspire me throughout the year.

"Choosing" the word is actually the last step of the process, to be totally forthcoming. There is a process: I sit in the quiet, I chat with Spirit, I Listen to what keeps coming up for me, and then – through discernment and revelation – the word is revealed to me. And then, I "choose" it.

I wrestle with the choosing of each year's word because of the loophole lesson I have agonizingly learned from my past word choices. If you've ever watched *Bedazzled*, the original film from 1967, you know what I'm talking about. The words I have chosen over the years all seem to be filled with great expectation and potential. And then, with the loophole of multiple meanings I did not consider, I end up getting kicked in the butt by my own word!

Words like "yielding" and "change" seemed like great words, until they led to painful changes and what felt more like a forced yielding. So, I have become much more cautious in my final choice, even after I have gone through the deep and spiritual process of Listening.

I feel like a good word for me, every year, is: Trust. And the mantra that goes with it is: Lean In.

Living with on-going issues of physical pain – along with depression – can feel like I am constantly doing battle with a beast.

Pain changes us. It has been changing me. The depression I do battle with has gained a major foothold. Crankiness, lack of patience, laziness, isolation, frustration, withdrawal – the whole gamut of demons and darkness – all of it has been surrounding and attacking me as I have been learning to live with pain.

And yet, because I am an Interfaith/Interspiritual Minister, I know better than to believe that this is happening without something else going on that I need to pay attention to, to learn from, to grow from. To Trust.

In 2010, I took the biggest trust fall of my life and went on a fifteen-day rafting excursion in the Grand Canyon. Rafting, on the Colorado River, with white water, rapids, me...I did this thing. It was an insane thing to do, something so far out of my comfort zone, there was no sign of that zone anywhere around! Not only did I leave my comfort zone, I kind of blew it up! It was a most magnificent experience, and not only did I survive, I learned a great deal about Trust.

There is a photo of me that was taken on day fourteen of the fifteen-day journey. One of our guides, Tracy, offered to let me take the oars. I was stunned to discover how heavy they were (solid wood) and how difficult the rowing was, even on a calm stretch of water. She trusted me with her boat, which meant a great deal to me. Of course, for the thirteen days before that, I had trusted her with my life. Also a pretty big deal.

I trusted Tracy (and the whole team of guides), I trusted the friends I was rafting with, I trusted the raft, I trusted the food, I trusted the river. And I learned to trust myself. Never before had I walked that kind of Trust Tightrope in the real world (the world outside of my own mind, a constant Trust Tightrope walk of intangible challenges).

This moment of taking the oars – captured in that cherished photo – was a triumphant moment for me. I showed that I was strong and courageous, willing, and, of course, humble enough to laugh at myself when I realized how strong Tracy had to be to have used those oars every day to keep us afloat.

Surely, now, as I move into another new year, facing on-going pain and the fears that seem to barnacle themselves to it, surely I can Trust that there is something here to be learned. That those who are trying to help me are doing the best they can. That those who love me are being as patient as they can be. That Maddie will forgive me for not walking her as much or as far as she might want. That this body has a Wisdom to it, a Divine Blueprint that Knows what Wholeness looks like, and it is working toward bringing that experience to the surface.

Trust. Lean In. My word and mantra.

We begin...now.

FEELING MY WAY THROUGH THE DARKNESS

It's just a story....it's all the past
Amazing me each day at how the time goes oh, so fast
From that window, feeling sure that I can't stay
Time traveling back and forth from then to where I'm living,
now, today

The ways that I have kept my self from leaving way too
soon
The words I use to convince my self
It'll all be ok

Don't give up....
It's just the journey
The darkness grows………..the seed

~ rev rachel hollander, today

To Be Human Again

You know it on the inside
So you should show it on the outside....
....Feet on ground....
And be human again
~ Aquilo, "Human"

Music goes directly to the deepest part of me. It cracks open the places I have sealed in concrete. It pours salt into the wounds I have tried to hide. It soothes the places that are raw and burned. It brings rain to the places that are the most arid deserts within me.

This song breaks me every time I listen to it. It breaks me in different ways:

It pushes me to question what I "know...on the inside."

It challenges me on what I choose to "show...on the outside."

It reminds me that there are others trying as hard as I am.

It encourages me to hold on during the most turbulent moments.

It allows me to cry from the depths of the pain.

It brings forth Gratitude that someone chose to share their creativity.

It awakens in me a sense of – dare I use the word – hopefulness.

It is one of the top five songs on my list of personal anthems.

It gives me a reason to continue.

Time

Even today, it is so very easy for me to slip back in time....It can happen in any moment, for no reason in particular....

It's my seventh-grade year. I'm about a week into classes at a new school (shifting from elementary to junior high), entering a new chapter of adolescence (moving from childhood to "tween"), finding my way with old and new friends coming together. And my dad – suddenly, without any warning – leaves me. It is a multilayered experience for me. I am a multilayered child.

It isn't "just" the death of a parent. It is the ending of safety, the ending of Love, the beginning of learning that nothing lasts and no one stays. My grief is untouchable. And it lasts longer than the other twelve-year-olds can understand.

At first, there is support and understanding. Then there is tolerant patience. And then they get tired of it, want it to stop, and interpret it as "attention-seeking." Truly, it is the opposite. If I had the option back then of disappearing, that would have been my choice. Attention was the last thing I wanted. It is still the last thing that I want.

I carry that experience with me still today. When I'm in the darkness, I wonder what the time limit will be for the support of those around me. How long can friends and family members deal with who I am? How long can supportive, encouraging friendship last? How much patience is enough patience? How long before understanding becomes annoyance? How much time is "enough" time for me to find my feet? What if I never do?

Surrender Versus Try

There are times when I look back at the experience of the hospital in NYC and wonder what my life would have been like had I simply surrendered. I was given that option, if not overtly by the doctors and hospital staff, then by the ongoing inner dialogue of fear and despair that rambled on relentlessly in my head. Why try? Life is hard. Bingo and pudding and a set schedule and no expectations are definitely alluring when the alternative appears to be an ongoing uphill battle. I began to make a mental pros-and-cons list based on my surrender-versus-try dilemma.

On the pro side of surrender: no effort necessary, always being taken care of, no longer a burden on my family (or anyone), pudding, bingo, art therapy, field trips, being around others like me who can't handle life, separation from the scary world.

On the pro side of try: freedom, choice, possibilities (at least in theory) for connection and work and a future, sunshine, family, friends, chocolate.

On the con side of surrender: no freedom of choice,

being on my own forever, isolation, loss of family and friends when they decide to stop visiting me (which I felt was inevitable), being "that" aunt.

On the con side of try: facing the unknown, walking through life alone, the potential for failure.

And on and on the discussions in my head would go.

Reflecting back on it now, I feel so much compassion for that version of me. She had no idea how wonderful – truly full of wonder – life could be, how amazing it would be to live across the road from the Pacific Ocean or to walk the streets of Assisi or to ride a rapid in the Grand Canyon. She didn't know how exciting it would be to love someone with all her heart, including having to let the relationship go, and still survive. She wouldn't have met all of her amazing nieces and nephews and watched them grow into phenomenal adults. She wasn't aware of the sweet animals that would become companions and guides to her over the years. She had no clue what songs were inside of her just waiting to be birthed into existence. And she could never have predicted how powerfully Spirit was going to act in and through her life.

Not knowing any of that, how could that young woman

find the courage within to decide to try? I truly have no idea. I just remember when I encountered Dr. Michael Shaffer – the first healer on my path back to life – when he first laid his healing hands on me and we spoke and he handed me Dan Millman's *Way of the Peaceful Warrior* and *2150 A.D.* by Thea Alexander, and the clouds in front of my eyes began to clear. I remember deciding, choosing, at that moment to allow healers, teachers, and guides to appear in my life. I stated that I was ready for them. And they showed up.

And then, after years of doing healing work, I realized that I have always had the choice to surrender, at any time, to the depression that still lives within me. This darkness doesn't go away. I found a place for it to live within me, a safe place that doesn't take up any more space than it is entitled to. The darkness is an important part of me. It is and always has been a great teacher.

I always have the choice to stop living the life I have co-created for myself. I can give up and go back to bingo and pudding anytime, if I so choose.

Once I recognized that I had that option, I felt a calm sense of comfort. It became part of the "safety net" of tools I had created. It is, of course, not my best or favorite option. It is always an option, though.

The Place of Not Knowing

I received two messages today from two different friends.

The first: "You can't hide from your inner shit. You can't sleep it off. You can't surgically remove it. You can't eat/buy/wish/exercise it away. You have to turn toward it and embrace it. Look into its eyes. Be patient and so very tender. Then get intimate with it until it shows you another way, a different you."

The second: "Do you have the patience to wait till your mud settles and the water is clear? Can you remain unmoving until the right action shows itself?" ~ Lao Tzu

I generally suck at patience. I like to know things, I like to plan, I like the safety net. I don't like to be in the dark in living situations, in relationships, in work environments, in health related -concerns- in pretty much any aspect of my life. Even in books. I will sometimes read the end of a book before I start it so

I know where I'm heading. Same with movies and TV shows: I want to know outcomes before I watch, so that I can relax and enjoy the journey.

I do not like to not know. I don't like the place of not knowing.

And yet that's where I live much of the time these days: in a place of not knowing. At various points in my life I have been an actor, an office assistant, a veterinary technician, a sign language interpreter, a student, and a minister. I have moved (A LOT!). I have loved, and I have lost. I have lived in Alaska, in California, in Idaho, and in upstate New York. I am now back in my hometown, reestablishing connections that remind me of my life from years ago. My personal identity is in flux. My work identity is in flux. My relationship identity is in flux. My place in this world seems to be almost entirely in flux.

Finding a way to be patient with change is challenging. Finding a way to be patient when the nature of that change is so uncertain….

I'm still learning.

A Balancing Act

I used to describe the difference between depression and happiness in this way: Depression was like a big, comfy recliner. Cushiony and soft, the kind I can sink into and feel completely enveloped, dressed in flannels, and with a big comforter wrapped around me. Safe, no risks, protected, comfortable.

While Happiness was like walking a tightrope with no net beneath me.

As I have continued walking my spiritual journey in life (which is inclusive of every other kind of walking I have done), I have had the opportunity to walk out on the tightrope – for stretches of time – while still keeping that recliner handy, just in case that "no-net scenario" became a bit too much for me. This creates two different experiences of balancing. There is the balance I must maintain when I am out on that tightrope, as well as balancing the times I choose to step out on it with the times I retreat to my recliner.

When I'm out walking on the tightrope, the balance is mostly about staying centered. Not too confident, not too exuberant. While also allowing myself the full experience of excitement and Gratitude. That balancing act is a continuous learning experience. I have found that if I get too cocky on that tightrope, I tend to stop paying attention to the focus needed to stay present on it, which can cause slippage, which can be very dangerous (no net, remember). To remain Grateful and Present gives me the centered balance to walk that tightrope with confidence and competence. The perfect balance.

Finding the balance between tightrope time and recliner time, well that gets a bit trickier. I'm one of those "give her an inch and she'll take a mile" types. One cookie is never as good as four cookies. One episode doesn't quite satisfy as much as binge-watching a whole season. An afternoon in the recliner can quickly and effortlessly become a day, a week, two weeks, a month...And the tightrope is forgotten as I sink deeper into the comfort of what is familiar. And safe.

On gray mornings, this becomes much more treacherous territory. It becomes way too easy to slide into the recliner and let the tightrope go for just one more day (which, as I've pointed out, can easily become much more than that one day).

The balancing act becomes an experience of negotiation: "You can have a recliner day as long as you do some laundry. Or read some homework. Or write a letter to someone. Or walk the dog (just a short walk, nothing dramatic). Or wash the dishes and make something legitimately healthy to eat. You can go back to the recliner between each of these. Or maybe just do one of them." And the negotiations continue on.

As a spiritual person living with depression, it is never just a "this or that" existence. I can't give up or give in. I've learned too much to allow that to happen.

So, it's a balancing act. The desire to withdraw to the recliner balanced with the commitment I've made to be in the world. The call of the bed and the blankets balanced with the Call of Life. The voice of "why even try" balanced with The Voice of Spirit (or whatever name you choose) that surrounds me in Love and Encouragement. The fear balanced with The Truth.

Nothing/Everything Is as It's Supposed to Be

These are the moments that completely flummox me.

After a few stellar days filled with gifts, blessings, friends, laughter, and possibility, I watch myself – as if I'm on a roller coaster – dive into the depths of sadness. Full-on tears, heartache, hopelessness, fear, darkness.

It's a surreal experience of feeling really good and hopeful and then feeling the "no" move in and over me like an expanding shadow. A sense of "No, don't step out onto the tightrope; things could go terribly wrong if you do."

I know it's important to have balance. Yin and Yang, the balance of all life, it's essential. Getting too excited, in my experience, tends to lead to a bit of letdown. The thing is that the balance of "possibility" shouldn't be misery.

I understand so much about myself, yet I don't understand where the truly deep sadness comes from. It comes from somewhere in the center of me and moves upward, outward and over me – a warmth, like lava, spreading slowly, and then, there it is, catching in the base of my throat. And the tears. Like a tsunami, they pour out of my eyes. It's confusing. Frustrating. Baffling. A little infuriating.

When I was younger, depression was like a big comfortable lounge chair recliner that I could curl up in. It was safe, protected, predictable, and familiar. Happiness was the thing to fear; it was a tightrope high up in the air. Risky. Insecure. No net.

That was my perspective for the longest time. And then it changed. A few years after I moved to Alaska, life became the safest and most thrilling tightrope walk ever. No net! I loved it! Happiness was how I lived, who I was, the way I walked.

And then, things changed again. I got sick, lost dear friends, struggled with work, watched my relationship fall apart. Being happy became dangerous again. Scary. Uncertain. A tightrope.

Now, as I am finding my footing again, I can see it. Clearly. Nothing is as it's supposed to be. And everything is as it's supposed to be.

Day to day, I don't know which will have the stronger pull: the recliner or the tightrope.

Questions with No Answers

I've always loved this quote by Rainer Maria Rilke: "I would like to beg you….to have patience with everything unresolved in your heart and to try to love the questions themselves as if they were locked rooms….Live the questions now. Perhaps then, someday far in the future, you will gradually, without even noticing it, live your way into the answer."

This is one of those "valid throughout my entire life" quotes. For some, those come from the Bible or some other holy book. Mine mostly come from song lyrics and letters written by those I admire. This one always hits right to the point, no matter what is happening.

It's a challenge for me, though, because, well, answers are what I want. I want to know why things happen the way they do. I want to know how someone I care about feels, what the important people in my life are thinking, what I should do next, where I fit in, when this pain will stop….please solve for x….

From algebra to human relationships, I still haven't figured out my way to any answers. It feels like a lot of fumbling in the dark.

True, the stakes aren't very high for algebra. They get increasingly higher with other people. And they are the highest when it comes to me.

What do I want?

Why am I here?

Why do I Love?

Why do I choose to experience the darkness rather than medicate it away?

Why did God plant the seed of Spiritual Vision within me?

How is it that every one of my role models is considered slightly mad or odd or "different" (and not in the "best" of ways), from an outsiders' opinion?

The questions I always end up with are much harder than "please solve for x."

There's no formula for those.

Fall

This season carries so much within it for me.

I remember feeling such a deep sense of melancholy – I don't think I used the word "depression" back then – when it was time to go back to school. I felt all the weight that that transition carried.

Fall will always be the time of my dad leaving the planet – that surreal moment that changed everything. I remember the way in which, just forty-eight hours before his death, we were all sitting in the family room of our house, singing and breaking the fast after Yom Kippur. Laughing and talking as if life would always be this way. Not knowing that in just two days, everything would change. Forever.

This season is that perfect mix of beauty and sadness.

I'm not a fan of summer, so it's not the sadness of losing the sunny, hot days. It is that moment of watching the leaves die. In the most magnificent way, with brilliant colors and the non-resistant acceptance of their release from the trees. Watching how nature takes care of itself; those leaves becoming part of the earth that will then feed the tree, the squirrels collecting and burying their acorns, the birds strengthening their nests.

It is a wistful sadness. A sweet sadness. The kind of sadness that is comforted by a warm blanket, snuggling with a sweet dog, sipping from a mug of hot cider, and feeling my dad's presence as I settle in to read and watch the leaves – and the world – transition outside the front window.

Wistful - an autumnal reflection

It's that time of year.

Actually, for me, that time of year starts around early September. That time of year that I can only identify as….Wistful.

The dictionary defines it as: "having or showing a feeling of vague or regretful longing."

The thesaurus gives us words to describe it like:

Contemplative. Mournful. Reflective. Nostalgic. Melancholy. Dreamy. Yearning.

September is the month my Dad died. It was sudden. I was young. It changed my life.

September was the beginning of the new school year. Hopeful. Filled with possibility. And a touch of dread.

October is harvest time, Halloween, candy corn, and temperatures getting cooler.

November is the time change, my best friend's birthday (he's no longer on the planet), the complicated experience of Thanksgiving.

And then there's the on-coming storm known as "The Holiday Season" which leads right into the ever-imposing New Year moment.

So much of my childhood, young adulthood, well, my life, really, is wrapped up in this time of year and, without realizing or anticipating it, I was overwhelmed with a feeling of wistfulness today.

I don't think I would call it "regretful longing," though. I don't much go in for regrets. Longing, sure. I can get on board with some longing. Not regretful though. Just….well, I think the thesaurus has it mostly right.

Melancholy. Nostalgic.

If my life was a movie, this time of year would be filled with sepia-tinted flashbacks. Moments of watching junior high soccer games and Halloween parties. Friday night skating. Choosing who I would fall in love with that year (confidently picking the one person who would never return my feelings).

New shoes and clean notebooks. Starting over and then, all too quickly, falling back into the patterns of "me-ness" that I couldn't seem to escape.

And "that song." It doesn't have to be a particular song. Just "that song," the one that – when I hear it – my soul kind of aches a little bit. And my heart groans just a little bit. That song brings a smile and some tears and…. memories.

As an adult, this time of year is all about sweaters and fireplaces, hot cider, wearing socks again. Putting away the summer stuff (light shoes, fans and A/C units) and breaking out the blankets, flannel sheets, and long-sleeved shirts.

Getting the new planner for the year ahead and writing in all of the birthdays and special dates I need to remember.

It's deeper than all of that, though. It's deeper than the time change and the loss of light.

Longing. The awareness of time passing. The awareness of the change in me. In my body. In my thoughts. In my perspective.

It's not as sad as it sounds. As I am writing this, it seems to sound somewhat sad and that was not my intention.

I just wanted to try and capture the feeling of wistfulness. It's not an easy essence to capture. Like most concepts, it's more like trying to capture the dust we see when the afternoon sun shines through the window. Or like the leaves that rained down from the trees today as I walked Maddie around the neighborhood. Can't really *catch* those things. Not with any kind of gracefulness, that is.

And now, with the world currently in quarantine, needing

to stay away and inside, the sense of wistfulness is feeling even more intense.

The "holiday season" is looking very different for some people. For me, not much is changing. It's been years since I have shared the holidays with friends or other people. There were those times, though….back then…. ah, again, the wistfulness…..

This feeling, this essence of "wistful," it seems to have a mind and agenda of its own. It shows up when it wants to and lingers as long as it feels like it.

In some ways, I dread it. And, in many other ways, I grieve when it decides that its good and ready to move on.

In the quiet, I wait.

Does It Have to Be This Hard?

I hear myself saying, "Nothing should be this hard" more and more these days.

I say it when I open a jar of pickles. I say it when I find

fleas on my dog – despite having spent an ungodly sum of money on the "guaranteed" treatments. I say it when untangling a shoelace, sitting in traffic, putting fitted sheets on the mattress...pretty much all the time.

I think what I'm really saying is that life shouldn't be so hard when it comes to just day-to-day living. Sure, I expect the big things to be tough: relationships, loving our enemies, struggling with the inequities in the world, forgiving what we feel is unforgivable. What about getting out of bed when it feels like there's just no point, though? Sometimes the simplest things are just that hard.

Do they have to be? Does everything have to be "this hard"?

Today, I decided to get rid of a piece of furniture. I just wanted it gone. So I jumped through some hoops, took some chances, and – ta-da! – the piece of furniture will be gone from my home tomorrow. That was not hard.

I swam today and had a peaceful experience doing it. As it should be. Easy.

I cherish these moments when things are easy. I acknowledge how blessed I am, in so many ways. I celebrate with gratitude and deep thankfulness. I try to let these moments fill me with the feeling that I can do it, this life thing. I can do it.

Even when all I really want to do is stay in bed.

What's Not on My Résumé

Functioning through heartache, also known as "smiling depression."

It's a skill, truly. Those of us who live with the darkness, the ever-present hum, have mastered this skill. It's how I live.

I can drive the car, do laundry, run errands, walk the dog, write a wedding ceremony, do what needs to get done, all while crying.

When running errands, the tears get put on "pause" while I go into the store, chat with the cashier, hold doors for folks, laugh, smile, and appear totally normal. Then, once back in the car, the tears return.

It's a perpetual sadness amid the gratitude. I am blessed

to have a car, to be able to fill it with fuel, to have a wonderful home (with a washer and dryer in it), a sweet and loving dog, a fridge with food, a clean bathroom, friends, acting talent (for my moments in the world)...on and on. There is SO much to be grateful for.

And there is the sadness, the darkness, the tears, the hum.

For some, this heartache, this pain, comes up in the in-between moments, like those times after they've been super busy and then they finish whatever it was that kept them occupied, or they go on vacation and just stop all the "doing." Or when a relationship that they've been in has gone to autopilot for a while and they finally leave it. It's in those moments, for most people, that the sadness comes up.

For me, it's constant. Even when things are going well or something good is happening, the hum is there. It never goes away. I simply have mastered how to function in and through it.

Smiling depression. If the world only knew what level of skill this requires.

Defining My Worth

I don't yet have all the right pieces of paper that prove my worth to the world — the certificates, the degrees. I'm working on it, though.

What I do have is more than five decades on this planet. Years of learning, growing, stumbling, getting back up, surviving, supporting, lifting, carrying, figuring out, solving, yielding, never giving up.

What I have is the ability to speak and write clearly and persuasively. The ability to truly listen. The ability to care. To want to help. To connect people. To lift them up.

I may never master algebra. Knowing how to solve for x is not going to make me a more valuable member of society. It's not my strength. It won't make me a better minister or a better friend, daughter, sister, neighbor, or employee. It won't make me smarter, stronger, more resilient, more committed, or more punctual.

And make no mistake: I am always punctual.

The Well

Sometimes I forget how to be unbroken. It feels like a faraway version of me that I can see and can never touch. It's like being in a mirror maze: There's an image of the whole me right there, in front of me, and yet completely untouchable.

To get through a day out in the world often requires filling my "in the world" fuel tank – at my inner well, my personal fuel station – when I am at home with just Maddie, not talking, just being in our cave. I fill it up with as much energy as I will need to be "on" for the length of time required.

When I'm out there, in the world, ministering, teaching, interpreting, socializing, I am my funny, friendly, and hardworking self. I talk, I give, I love, I share.

Authentically. I am not faking or lying in the way I show up in those moments.

After a few hours, though, I feel my fuel start to run low, and once I'm safely back in the car, I cry on the drive home.

It doesn't feel like a sustainable system. The fact that I give away my stores of energy is not necessarily a good thing. The fact that I can keep digging deeper to find more to give, without my well ever seeming to fully fill back up, may not be the best way to move through life. And yet what choice do I have? It's a cycle of feeling empty, needing to give, finding ways to give, feeling more empty, needing to give more, finding more ways to give, and on and on.

My processes for refilling the well don't always work. When they don't, I face the ongoing challenge of being tempted to surrender to life in the darkness.

The thing is, I don't surrender. I do keep showing up, as much as I can. I perform my life as best as I can. And I discover how, miraculously, each day my well gets filled enough to make tomorrow possible.

Stubbornness

When I'm in the depths of depression, I feel that I'm all alone.

I acknowledge the "fact" that I am not. My mom is 6.2

miles from me. Friends are just a text or a phone call away. Facebook pals are always there. And, of course, Maddie is right here, ready to snuggle. I am not alone.

And....

I am not going to call anyone, text anyone, post on Facebook, reach out, or let anyone know how deep I have sunk into the darkness. It's just not going to happen.

What am I going to say? "It's happening...again"? There aren't any words for what I feel. There are too many words for what I feel. There are too many feelings for what I feel.

The thought of waking someone up, interrupting a date night, disrupting family time, messing up someone's plans for a quiet afternoon...this horrifies me. I won't ever do it.

It's not a lack of gratitude, I promise. My heart aches with how grateful I am for the friends, family, friends who are family, strangers who are friends – all of the folks who show up in my life. I

In a way, it's *because* of that gratitude that I won't

interject my darkness into their lives. Your lives. I don't want to.

Plus, there isn't anything that anyone else can do. No one can make it go away. Yes, there are moments when others shine some light into the darkness and dispel its shadow for a moment or two. It comes back, though. And I don't want anyone to think they've failed to help me. I couldn't take that.

Todd Rundgren nailed this experience in a song called "If I Have to Be Alone":

And if nobody understands
That special creature that is me
Then no one else knows truly what it is
To be alone...

Jimmy and I used to sit together and listen to this song and just stare into space, without words, taking it in, feeling it. Jimmy understood. His absence is a constant reminder of what being alone feels like for me.

Because I do feel alone. Even in the moments of knowing that I'm not.

The Valley of the Shadow

One does not become enlightened by imagining figures
of light, but by making the darkness conscious.
~ Carl Jung

In the Twenty-Third Psalm - " though I walk through the
valley of the shadow of death, I fear no Evil, for you are
with me" - many of us forget to focus on the part about
"walking through." We are *walking through* the valley of
the shadow. We're not having a picnic or setting up a
tent and camping there. We're walking through it.

There are two points here that I use as reminders for
myself. One is to keep walking. The other is to not feel
crappy about where I'm walking. Or the fact that I am
walking it...again. OK. That's a third point.

I am not alone. Everyone is doing this walk, at one time or
another. It's never about how long we linger in the valley,
how slow we choose to walk, or what route we choose to
take through it — or sometimes around it. Why do I judge
this as a "bad thing"?

The fact is, at least once in our lives, we walk it. Some of us walk it more often than others.

So that quote from Carl Jung....it arrived just in time.

We learn about ourselves, we grow, we change, we connect with others, and we find our way through by making the darkness visible...by bringing our darkness to the light. So, maybe walking through the valley of the shadow means bringing light *into* the valley of the shadow. Maybe it's not so much about trudging through this dark valley, this dark night of the soul, this dark pain just trying to get to the light. Maybe it's about remembering that we carry the light....We carry the light.

In Jewish temples there's an Eternal, Everlasting Light that shines over the ark where the Torah is kept. I always used to think, "Don't we all have one of those? Don't we all have an Everlasting Light inside of us?" As long as we're alive, I believe that we do. I truly believe that I do.

Even today. Even as I walk through the valley of the shadow. Even during this dark night of the soul. I carry the Light. I am not alone.

What Do You Want?

Oftentimes, when I am walking through the valley of the darkness, I've been asked, "Well, what do you want to feel?"

Sometimes it gets even more basic than that. When I am asked, "What do you want?" I don't always have an answer. Or my answer is "too big" for me to put into words.

I was asked this yesterday. Here was my response:

What I want...

I want to Love.

I want to graduate from college with a 4.0.

I want to live (and be financially supported) as a minister.

I want that aspiration to not be so hard to achieve.

I want Maddie to live forever.

I want to get through the dark times with more God and less pain.

I want to be Loved for who I am.

I want to balance my total acceptance of being alone with also knowing that those I love are there.

I want to find that place where the Love I have to give, "belongs."

Sometimes I want a conventional relationship.

Sometimes I want to be totally on my own, answering to no one.

Sometimes I want to shop for two.

Sometimes I want to buy ready-to-spread frosting and just say, "enough already" to everything.

I want to be smarter.

I want life to be easier.

I want my book to be published, and I want it to be read.

I want my mom to always See me as I am.

I want my dad (and Jimmy and Carl and Amy and Michael and Steven and Eddie and Alan Rickman) to be alive.

I want to understand everything while also maintaining the Mystery.

I want my own personal lap pool.

Sometimes I want to kiss someone.

Sometimes I want no one to get close enough to me to kiss.

I want enough money so that I never have to worry and to still have enough to help others.

I want to effect change in the world.

I want to help others AND myself.

I want some things to never change.

I want some things to absolutely change.

I want the Truth to not hurt.

I want to never hurt another person.

I want to not get hurt.

I want good neighbors.

I want my tires to keep me safe.

I want to eat chocolate, sugar, bacon, pasta, cheese and whatever I want without any repercussions.

I want to be thin.

I want to accept myself as I am.

I want to be healthier (without "suffering" or deprivation).

I want to not want intimacy.

I want intimacy with Safety and Love.

I want to be courageous all of the time.

I want ignorance to be shaken awake.

I want to be understood the way I understand myself.

I want to always remember who I Truly Am.

"Why Don't You Call Someone?"

As I sat in the dark place, feeling the tears literally stinging my eyes, the familiar ache creeping up, the pressure on my chest, I was asked by someone I love, "Why don't you ask for help? Why don't you call someone?"

Because I can't.
Because it doesn't change anything.
Because within just a few moments, I will feel that recurring need to take care of them because of how bad they feel for me.
Because it's frustrating.
Because it's humiliating.
Because I don't want to.
Because, in the end, it doesn't help.
Because they may say, "Not now, I'm busy."
Because they might say, "I'm so sorry."
Because they may not know what to say (and then I feel stupid).

Because I know it will pass.
Because there's nothing wrong with what I feel...

There's nothing wrong with what I am feeling. Why is this experience labeled as "bad"? Why do I think it's bad? If God is in the happy moments, in the proud moments, in the triumphant moments, in the grateful moments, in the sweet moments, then isn't God in this moment, too?

Isn't that what I teach, that God is in/with us in every moment of our lives?

I don't reach out because I am not down a well.
I did not run out of gas on the highway.
I don't have a flat tire.
I haven't lost Maddie.

I am home, in my house, warm and safe and fed. With music and technology and Maddie. I have comfortable clothes, socks that fit perfectly, flannel sheets...

I don't call someone because I know what this is. I know it won't last. I know what helps. I know I am never alone.

I take the next breath...

Relationships 101

Relationships can be challenging even for the most emotionally and psychologically healthy of folks. For someone like me, they're like a minefield of possible emotional and social explosions.

Beginning, cultivating, maintaining, and surviving intimate relationships can become a Mount Everest climbing expedition for those of us who live with – and wrangle – depression. Not only are we working hard to care for ourselves, to keep ourselves healthy and somewhat "normal," we also want to show up fully in the relationship. This can be challenging on a few fronts, balancing the inner and outer experiences of being with another person. It can look kind of like this:

1. Protecting. Shielding them from our bouts of darkness, hiding from them our moments of sadness, becoming super creative in our explanations of "what's wrong" when there's nothing specifically wrong ("No, seriously, it really is me, and not you, this time").

2. Second-class citizen-ing. Continuously putting our "stuff" on the back burner because our partner is dealing

with "real" challenges. These comparisons can become deadly. Our "stuff" IS real. Very real. It just may not seem as real as our partner's job issues or physical health issues or even their frustrations with us.

3. Excusing/justifying, part I. Personal example: I am not a hiking kind of person. My former partner was. When I would pass on offers to go hiking, I was told that I was "feeding into" the depression and not doing anything to make myself feel better. I had to explain that: (a) I didn't like hiking to begin with, and (b) there was no way that hiking was going to make me feel better. Add to this the physical pain that I was experiencing that made even walking unpleasant. So, I would find myself creating stories, excuses, reasons for not being able to join in the outdoor excursions. The upside of this? I got A LOT of laundry done!

4. Excusing/justifying, part II. After a while, bowing out of social events because the depression makes it too difficult may no longer be an "acceptable" reason. We feel the need to create headaches that don't exist or fabricate stories about why we can't attend because of this person or that location or whatever. Honesty seems to stop mattering. The thing is, if we were exhausted from chemotherapy, there'd be no discussion or resistance.

The darkness is not always accepted as an equally legitimate reason for needing to withdraw from social situations.

5. Carrying our weight, and more. Having a relationship end because we couldn't show up fully – for whatever reason, maybe fear of the rejection of our true selves – becomes yet another piece of baggage we carry. It's "our fault" that things didn't work out. We're broken and so we must have broken the relationship. It must be our fault; it must be us. It couldn't possibly be because our partner didn't truly see us or try to understand. Or, if they did, we can excuse that away quickly by remembering that we just made it that much harder for them, so no matter how much they tried, we just made it way too difficult. We drained them. We depleted them. We, we, we...

We forget that we are worthy of love.

Read that sentence again. Go ahead. I'll wait!

That we are worthy of patience and understanding. We are worthy of the same exact kind of compassion and patience and understanding we would give to someone like us who we knew needed it.

And, the most frightening of all:

6. Revealing our true selves. As a relationship begins to deepen, we hear from our partner: "I want to know everything about you; I want to KNOW YOU." We believe them. We think, "Wow! I've finally met that person who really does want to know me, who I can let in, who will be safe to be fully real with." And so, maybe not all at once, we begin to let them see our not-so-cheerful side, our not-always-okay self. And at first, there might be a sweet, superficial understanding of who we are. Maybe they think it's only momentary or that it can't be as bad as we say. As we become more comfortable and feel safer, we reveal more. And then, there's the moment it turns. The "why are you like that?" questions begin. The "when will you get over this?" questions. The "just stop it" demands. The "fine, I'm going without you" moments. And, finally, the "I can't deal with you" that we've feared – and always knew – would come.

Rescue Mission

A long time ago, I wanted to be rescued from my life. I was struggling with the depression, not doing well. I was lonely. I was feeling un-seen, un-wanted, un-needed.

I was afraid of the future. My future. I had no idea what was going to happen to me.

I just wanted to be rescued.

So, I fell in love.

And then I fell in love again.

And then, I did it again...Noticing a pattern here?

It's not that I didn't truly love the people I fell in love with. I did. I also, however, really wanted to be rescued. I wanted them to love me so that I would *be* loved.

Being loved meant that I would be taken care of. I would never be lonely. Someone would be there whenever I needed them. When my car ran out of gas or the dishwasher backed up. Or there was a spider in the bathroom. Or there was a noise outside at night.

The problem was, I didn't really *want* someone there all of the time. I really liked having my own space, my own way of doing things, hanging photos on the wall, eating chips for dinner, waking up in my own way.

Hence, the dilemma:

Be alone, and therefore not rescued.
Or
Find someone who would love me, not live with me (or, at least not be in my space all the time). More than a roommate, less than a clingy romance. Someone who liked to kiss (and not much more than that). A social-event date who would be *with* me and yet wouldn't hover over or suffocate me.

Bonnie Raitt has a song that says: "One part be my lover, one part go away."

That. I wanted that. A part-time rescuer.

I spent years working on this issue, this problem, of mine. The "rescue mission" addiction. And I thought I had gotten past it. I really did. Recently, I began to feel stronger, more clear, happier, more solid. I thought, well, that's one thing checked off the "Rachel needs to fix this crap" list.

And then...I was feeling really cranky. Edgy. Frustrated. I couldn't understand what it was from. Maybe the pandemic. Maybe school. Over-extending myself as a minister, possibly. Well, it could have been any of those. Maybe it could have been all of those. As well as...

I discovered that I had recently cast someone in my life into the role of rescuer. Without noticing it (because that's how the most dangerous part of my brain works), some idea of this person as a rescuer had snuck right into my psyche and set up camp.

Sitting on my bed yesterday, I started crying as a song I love started playing from my phone. And, whammo! I said, out loud, "You just assigned that person the rescue mission. How could this happen?!?"

The first feeling was complete disappointment. In my self. How could I have allowed that to happen? How could that thought have crept back into my brain without my knowing? Without my permission? And why? Why, why WHY has it returned? I don't want it. I don't like it. I don't believe it.

Wait...Do I? Do I want someone to rescue me? Is that such a bad thing to want? Does it make me weak? Does it make me less-than?

Hold up, monkey mind! In order:

No.
No, I don't.
Yes, it is.
Yes, it does.
Yep. Sorry, Sister.

If I really wanted to - intimately - share my life with someone, that would be one thing.

If I really felt like that was something I was capable of doing, that would be acceptable.

If I really saw my future as one I could share with someone - on equal footing - who accepted me with all of my quirks (and I, with theirs), then, well...It would happen.

It would be happening. And it isn't.

Here's the lifeline, though (did you honestly think I'd leave you hanging with that hopeless thought?!?). Well, before I tell you the lifeline, here's how I got to it. I woke up again. Today. In my home. With my dog. Listening to the wind blowing outside. Snuggled into my bed. Me. And my dog.

And I was happy. Because I remembered the lifeline:

In every moment, with every breath, as I allow each thought to come through, I can choose again. I can choose to rescue myself.

I can reconnect to the truth of who I am. I can swoop in, right on time, and be my own rescue mission. For my self.

No more sense of failure. No more feeling bad about slipping back into an old thought pattern. No more edgy crankiness. No more beating myself up. No regrets.

Rescued. I can rescue myself. As many times as I need, whenever I need.

This is a good thing to know.

Being Ourselves

Sometimes being ourselves is tricky.

When I say, "Well, I'm just being myself," what do I actually mean? Because my "self" can be different at different times. My "self" in a social situation is more social! More outgoing, more gregarious, more involved and engaged.

And when I'm my "self" at home, when I'm just hanging out with Maddie, that's more quiet and introspective. It's more like cave time: a little isolating — not in a bad way, just in a way that lets me retreat from the world.

I wrote a song a few years ago called "The Big Reveal," where somebody was saying to me, "Well, this is who I am, and you have to love me for who I am!" And my lyric was, "You say, 'This is who I am, love me for who I am, and that's not always so easy to do.'" And the truth is it isn't always easy to love others when they say, "This is who I am, love me!" It's also not easy to love myself, or to ask someone else to love me when I say, "Well, this is who I am, love me."

And yet, that's all we really want. To be Seen (capital S) and Loved (capital L) for Who We Truly Are, Our Selves.

There are these photos that my soul twin, Jimmy, took of me years ago (YEARS ago!) in an old apartment I lived in (that I loved). He wanted to do a photo shoot for a class he was taking. In each of these photos, I am my Self. And yet, each one of them is a very different version of my "self." I'm laughing, I'm serious, I'm vulnerable, I'm a bad-ass, I'm...a little guarded. And that's all "me."

And so as we move through our lives, the tricky part is, how do we stay ourselves and BE ourselves without pushing others away with those words "THIS IS WHO I AM: LOVE ME OR LEAVE ME!" How can we say, "This is who I am: I am worthy of being Loved." This is who I am: "SEE me (capital S). See me for who I am. And (capital L) Love me, whether you like me or not."

This is the big lesson I'm pondering currently. How to be in this world, and be myself, and find Love, in whatever form. Because I will say that Maddie Loves me, just as I am, in all the different forms that I am – EXCEPT when I'm crying! She doesn't want to be around me when I'm crying! (That's another story.)

Just figuring out how to BE ourselves: find who we are, express who we are, Love our Selves for who we are, show up AS we are. And find our place, find where our piece in the Cosmic Puzzle fits AS we are. AND be open to expanding who we are, and changing who we are, and finding new ways of expressing who we are...My God, it's LIMITLESS! It's limitless. So, maybe it can be enough to just Know for today that we are Seen. And we are Loved. Maybe only by ourselves. We can let that be enough.

Feeling Broken

> There is a crack in everything
> That's how the light gets in"
> ~ Leonard Cohen, "Anthem"

Paulo Coelho also writes about this in a story with an old man explaining that his old, beat-up heart is more beautiful than a "new and perfect" heart.

He shares that, as he gave away his heart, some people returned it with a piece missing, causing the heart to be damaged, to have holes. Without shame, he declares that those empty spaces remind him of the moments when he gave his love. And that the giving of love is always a risk. Always a risk worth taking.

He ends the story by saying, "I hope someday they may return and fill the space I have waiting. So now do you see what true beauty is?"

It's a real challenge to not feel broken all of the time.

And to not see - and judge - brokenness as wrong or
bad.

From the feeling of not quite fitting in, even with friends
or my own family sometimes, to feeling:

forgotten and unseen
like the one not chosen
like the crazy one (and fulfilling that image)
like something is always being missed ("but I told you,"
"but I already explained that to you," "we already talked
about that," "why do you still think that?")
like a burden
like there are things I can never have (understanding,
patience, security)
like the one who is a pain to deal with
like people are getting tired of it
like no one will ever understand
like everyone will always leave
like anything said is the wrong thing
like it's never worth it
like "alone" is all that is awaiting

It's not something I want to feel. And there are moments
— those amazing, triumphant, fleeting moments — when I

don't feel that way, when I don't feel any of it.

It is in the moments of awareness that someone important could leave because of how I feel and how the darkness expresses itself. In those moments, I feel the most broken. And I don't want to. And I do. And it is what it is, awareness or not.

It's this frustrating and terrifying cycle:

I feel broken.
I don't want to.
Someone cares.
I show them.
They understand.
Until they don't.
I hide it so they won't leave.
They want me to be authentic.
I am.
They get impatient.
I try to be real while trying to control it.
It doesn't work.
They say they don't like/understand it.
I feel shame (on top of everything else).
I can't express myself.
They get frustrated.

I get frustrated.
They leave.
I think, "yeah, this is how it's supposed to be."
I feel broken.

This hurts so deeply. So, I look for ways to remind myself that broken doesn't mean bad or wrong or less than.

There is a process in Japan called Kintsugi (*Kintsukuroi*, which means "golden repair"). When a piece of pottery is broken, it is put back together using gold to fuse the broken places. The idea is to emphasize, to own, the places of brokenness, instead of attempting to hide them or feel ashamed of them. To make them even more beautiful, stronger, and give them a new life.

This is what Coehlo was talking about in that story of the old man and his not-so-perfect heart.

Many teachers, writers, mystics have written about the beauty in being broken, the perfection in being imperfect. Wayne Muller, Henri Nouwen, Fr. Richard Rohr, Saint Teresa of Avila, Brother Francesco, Rumi, Sister Helen Prejean....

It hurts to feel broken. It hurts to feel torn apart.

It helps to know that somewhere in all of it, there is beauty. That, as Mr. Cohen sang, the brokenness creates a space for the light to come in.

There is a reason I am here. Broken as I am. And, as I am, I try. I stay.

Immobilizing Squirrel

Sometimes I manage to work it out so that I have "no time" to do the things I need to do. It's actually quite ridiculous; I have all the time I need. And, still, the depression is immobilizing and very focused on making me comply.

Getting out of bed is often the most difficult moment of the day. Fortunately, I have a dog with certain needs, and she can only hit the snooze with me for so long. Even so, I make a mental deal with myself that if I get up and take her out, we can always go back to bed. We don't do that. It's just one of the necessary negotiation points that arise almost every day.

Once the morning Maddie walk is complete, I make my way to the couch. Before I can start anything productive like writing or working, first I search for the best show on the nearest listening device (preferably an old-time radio stream. *Gunsmoke* is always a first choice. After that, the dramas will do, or *Yours Truly, Johnny Dollar, Richard Diamond,* maybe *The Saint*.) Then it's a quick check of e-mail or Facebook on the laptop. Next is finding something reasonable to eat and drink. (Reasonable food is rarely breakfast-like. I'm usually swayed by convenience, and leftovers work just fine.)

I'll start working and might get distracted by IMDb movie trailers and YouTube videos. No idea how that happens, and yet it happens so easily. And even while I'm doing it, I recognize what's happening. I might be thinking, "Wow, Rachel. You were in the middle of writing and now you're watching movie trailers to movies that you won't ever go to the theatre to see." Nice, right? Incorporating hopelessness and mocking self-criticism with the agoraphobia I experience into one simple sentence. One thing's for sure: I'm better at being mean to me than anyone else could ever be.

Depression is both immobilizing and kind of like the character Dug in the movie *Up*. Dug is a dog distracted by squirrels. (If you haven't seen the movie, do. Just trust me. Go watch it.) Any "squirrel" will do to keep me from being in the present moment because the present moment can usually be scary, confusing, possibly empty, unknown, isolating, dark, and uncomfortable.

Role Models

Why am I so hard on myself? I can absolutely crush myself with criticism. I'm better at it than anybody else.

Why am I like this?

My wonderful therapist Sarah used to ask me that same question. And my simple answer was that it kept me humble, kept me from buying into my own made-up stories and excuses. My role models were equally hard on themselves – not as unkind as I am, I don't think, but still quite demanding, impatient, and intolerant of weakness. Yet each one of them had such powerful weaknesses that made them more real. That's why I love them. That's why they are my role models. I call them my Soul Team.

Who is on my Soul Team? There are several folks, both real and fictional.

Here are the top five:

Brother Francesco. Saint Francis of Assisi always felt like he was not enough for God, that he could always DO more and BE less.

Mother Teresa. She felt that she had completely lost her faith and that God had abandoned her.

Vincent van Gogh. He only wanted to be a pastor and serve God and yet felt like a failure – to God and as a painter.

Joan of Arc. Even she had a moment of doubt in an attempt to save her own life.

Brother Lawrence. Carmelite Monk who discovered God in every action, every moment, every task, every breath, throughout his day.

All five of these souls were the embodiment of what they thought they weren't. Just like the characters in *The Wizard of Oz* (my favorite movie and ultimate go-to metaphor for life).

So, by beating myself up, does that mean I'm actually

okay? It sure sounds like I'm making the case for that. At the same time, as an individualized expression of The One, who am I to tear myself apart? Would I stand at the Grand Canyon and think, "Well, God sure could have done better with THIS." Or look at the *David* and say, "Hmm...not sure he got the feet quite right." Why is it okay to rip apart the creation that is *me* if I wouldn't do that to someone else or some other part of creation I think is magnificent?

This is what depression does. It's what it is. Questioning everything. Doubting everything. Casting darkness on what should or could be lit up like the sun. Making true what isn't the truth. Making real what isn't reality.

Creating stories of failure and pointlessness when what is actually happening is simply a moment that is calling for patience and the embracing of unknowing.

Reasons to Stay

In the mid-1990s I had a true turning point, a surreal moment when life reflected back at me, showing me what I could do with how I had changed, what I had learned. Proving to me it's worthwhile to keep showing up.

I was on tour with a theatre company that performed in both ASL (sign language) and spoken English. There were both deaf and hearing company members. We were spending the night in a motel in Jacksonville, Florida. My roomie was a deaf, male actor in the company. We had settled in for the night after having heard some loud noises from the room next door. I was relieved when they stopped and we could get some sleep.

We were watching the news when I heard a woman's voice, a whimpering sound, coming from outside the room. We were on the third floor of the motel, one of those where the doors lead directly to the outside with a balcony overlooking the parking lot. I muted the TV and listened again. My roomie had his hearing aids out so he didn't hear it. It was clearer now, a woman's voice crying, saying the words, "Help me. Help. I don't want to do this." In my pajamas, I opened the door a bit and saw her. The woman was perched like a bird on the railing overlooking the parking lot, preparing to throw herself off. I stepped out, cautiously, and began to talk with her.

She explained that the man in the room next door to us had broken her heart, he had lied to her, and now he wouldn't open the door. In fact, he had "moved on" from her to another date and was long gone for the night. As I approached her slowly, I heard myself saying things to her about the value of life, how no man was worth dying for, and how she had so much more to look forward to. These and more words that had been said to me so many times before came pouring forth from me. All spoken gently – and with more authentic honesty than I could have ever imagined myself being capable of – as I moved closer to her.

She was saying that she didn't really want to jump, however, in the position she was in physically, she didn't see an "out." By that time, I had reached her and - with her permission - carefully placed my hand on her back. I advised her to lean into my hand, to relax backward. She was crying and panicked and yet, with a breath, she leaned back and I caught her in my arms.

She fell into me, sobbing, and I held her and told her everything would be alright. The police had arrived by this time, and they took her away.

After a few hours of restless sleep, there was a knock on

our door at 5:00 a.m. The motel manager and the front desk clerk were there with a certificate of thanks from the motel for what I had done.

There are moments when we get to give back. When it all suddenly makes sense, even just for a moment. I promise you, they are worth the wait.

Facing the Fire

I recently joined in with a group of friends at a guided glass-blowing experience. The three artisans explained the process, showed us the tools and the ovens (heated to over two-thousand degrees), and then, with care and humor and support, they guided us to create our own masterpieces. Within our group there were some who were wary (or just outright frightened!) of the heat and the potential danger. Some were curious and excited about what would happen. Some were ready to dive right in and create. And, for me, I was most concerned about being able to participate due to a temporary physical limitation.

Curiosity and Courage seemed to be the themes of the day. Pushing ourselves past our comfort zones, facing the heat without fear, facing our fear with support and encouragement.

And yielding to those who had the skill, knowledge, experience, Wisdom, and Compassion to guide us through.

There was humor, of course! And cheering, with authentic Love and caring friendship for one another.

This is life, right? I mean, look at it:

Each day we step out our doors and face the heat and potential dangers, excitements, surprises, and risks of the world outside of our beds. We seek Guidance and Support from others. We appreciate encouragement and support from those around us. We hope to find humor and joy in as many moments as possible. We push ourselves past our comfort zones at work, in relationships, with family, in traffic, at the post office, online, anywhere we encounter other people (or ourselves) in ways that are not familiar or "easy."

And we learn new ways of creating, of co-creating, our lives. We discover that we can make something beautiful from something broken. We can take the melted-down mess of our lives and reshape it into something that glimmers in the light. Something we can be proud of, share with others, and look at with Loving Sweetness and say, "I made this."

We can come through the fire, and we can shine. Still breakable, yet stronger than before. Resilient, fragile, radiant, delicate...Perfectly imperfect. In our own way.

Etiquette, in the Darkness

I've learned that my experience of sadness is totally mine and doesn't need to oppress or impact others. It's not about faking or hiding it or feeling any sense of shame about it. It is about the simple humanity of not desiring to throw up my darkness onto people who don't need or deserve to have that happen to them. They are trying as hard as I am to get through their day, their life. They don't need excess weight to drag them down.

Yesterday, I was feeling a resurgence of the sadness tsunami that has been rolling over me lately. It comes out of nowhere, washes over me and completely knocks me down, and then rolls on back out to wherever it lives. The tricky piece was that it happened while I was in the grocery store.

I love my neighborhood grocery store. Every employee is genuinely upbeat and friendly. Most of the shoppers are as well. It's like a little slice of carefree happiness whenever I go in there. I didn't feel it was necessary to bring out my inner Eeyore and cast gloom all over the folks in there just trying to do their shopping or get their work done.

Years ago, I struggled with being fake, with pushing my real feelings down so deep and covering them with outlandish, obnoxious, and overcompensating lunacy that no one — sometimes not even me — knew what I was actually feeling. I made a promise to myself many years ago that I would not do that again. That even if it was uncomfortable, I would be authentic in my emotional experience.

The difference is this: As I moved through the store, I would feel the sadness and tears well up in the canned veggies aisle. I would allow the feeling to rise. I would breathe. And then move along. In the next moment, at the deli counter, when the woman serving me so kindly asked about my tattoo and called me "darlin'" and was telling me about her cooking plans for the weekend, I was attentive and happy to engage with her. Truly happy.

After leaving her, and heading for the applesauce, I could feel the sadness wave coming back in. I let it. And then, in the checkout lane, I experienced a sweet and funny exchange with the woman working the register.

After leaving the store, sitting and crying in the car, I had one more stop to make. At that stop, a woman and I laughed about how ice cream is essential, no matter the weather. As I drove home, the tears returned.

There was no denying that the sadness and the darkness were present. There was also absolutely no need for me to ruin anyone else's day with it. And, in each of those exchanges, I wasn't faking my smile or my laughter or my engagement.

I was simply allowing each moment to be what it was,

without any attachment to it.

I knew the sadness would return. It always does. I was so very grateful for those joyful moments because they were gifts to me. They were light in the darkness. I was real in those moments. I gratefully accepted them as offerings, generous offerings of spirit. I embraced them and let them pass. Just as I allowed the darkness to work through me, letting it pass as well.

Sometimes I forget that the darkness will pass. Sometimes it doesn't feel like it ever will.

Even if it didn't ever pass, though, there's no reason for me to overhwelm others with it. They have their own sadness and struggles to move through. Sometimes, most times — maybe all the time — it's best to gift each other with the passing moments of laughter and connection, regardless of what is happening inside of us. It's not faking anything. It's simply showing kindness.

Morning Text Ministry

It started because of an article I read. There was a man in New York City who died, and no one knew for more than two weeks. He had no friends, no family, no connections with anyone else. He died alone and was "found" more than two weeks after his death.

I told my friend Harvey about this because we were both living alone and he was in NYC and, truth be told, I worried about him. So, we started this morning text check-in thing. I would text him when I woke up, and he would text back, so we both knew that we were alive.

Texting with him each morning on our drive from Alaska to Ithaca, NY became an essential part of the journey.

Once I arrived in Ithaca, I started experiencing this disturbing nighttime anxiety, a fear that if I died during the night, who would take care of Maddie? So, I asked my beloved friend Joan (who lived about fifteen minutes away) if I could also text her in the morning, just to confirm that I woke up. She lovingly agreed to do this with me. It was just the two of them at this point.

And then, it expanded. Other friends who live alone, who might not have anyone checking in on them, who feel somewhat isolated, or who just don't always wake up feeling so great, became part of this new morning text ritual.

It became what I call the Morning Text Ministry. Friends in my town, in Alaska, Florida, New York, Colorado, Connecticut, Washington State, and one who is always on the road traveling...all have become part of this beautiful "family." We check in, we lift each other up, we make each other laugh a little, we make sure that we're doing okay (and if we're not, we help each other through whatever moment is happening).

Some folks call this Intentional Community. I like to think of it as a lifeline, to remind us that we don't have to feel totally alone, like no one is out there caring about whether or not we woke up.

There's always room for one more! Just sayin'.

Demons on Paper

There was a time when just the mere idea of putting the secret stories of the demons on paper would have paralyzed me. They had their own rules for my life, their own way of handling me. The simple thought of exposing them, in black and white, would have meant instant and painful retaliation.

They were always there, since I was very young. I didn't have a name for them or even an image to attach to them; I just felt them...and heard them.

Then, sometime in the mid-1980s, I read a book called *This Present Darkness* by Frank Peretti. It is Christian fiction, and had I known that, I might never have read it. It was gifted to me, though, by someone I respected, so I did. In that book, there were demons, the representation of evil. The description of them was perfect. It was almost as if someone had seen what I had been living with for so long.

Large, shiny black, greasy, terrifying flying things with sharp talons and huge wings. Not like that sweet toothless dragon from *How to Train Your Dragon*. No, these are closer to The Red Knight from *The Fisher King*, except with huge wings, claws, and...greasy.

Once I had been given that visual, it was nearly impossible to keep these demons at bay, to have any kind of strength against them or show any resistance to them. When I wrote or told anyone about them, there was an egotistical, cocky pride that rose up in them. It was as if they enjoyed the attention, regardless of it being negative attention.

Now, so many years later, I can see that they were part of the world I created to try to understand what I was living with and doing battle with, how I was trying to just stay alive. I needed visuals. I needed characters. I needed antagonists – outside of myself – to make it less about what might be wrong with me medically and more about my failings as a human being. A separation between my active choices and my "predestined fate." The demons, and this line of thinking, kept me powerless.

As long as I was powerless, I didn't have to do anything to change. I didn't have to try. I could stay a victim to the feelings, the terror, the demons, the darkness.

Learning how to stand up was a process. It wasn't a linear journey, like a plane taking off. It was more like a person learning how to walk again after a stroke. Frustrating, infuriating, with moments of small triumphs and backsliding, feeling encouraged and defeated at the same time, desiring and accepting help from friends while also wanting to do it myself, wanting to be "all better" right away while still recognizing that the journey is more important than the destination.

There may not be actual demons anymore, something I am truly grateful for. I still live moving in and out of and through the darkness. I always will. It's my journey, this time around.

That's why it was such a challenge to finish this book. Because the journey – my story – continues.

Survival Liar

There are times when it feels like I have lost the ability to actually know and identify how I feel because I've lied about it so much and for so long.

"Lying" might seem too harsh a word for what I did. And yet, it *is* what I did. I protected myself, I diverted the focus, I disguised my vulnerability, I survived, and I did it by saying what needed to be said, what I thought would make sense, what I thought would keep me safe, what I thought people wanted to hear, what would make the moment pass easier.

As a child, I lied about how I was feeling because I was afraid of what the response would be if I told the truth (i.e., if I expressed my disappointment or anger, others might get angry with or at me. Or leave).

After my dad died, I lied to the child psychologist because there was no point in telling her the truth. She couldn't bring my dad back. What could she possibly do to help me?

In eighth grade, I stopped crying and lied about how I really felt because I was afraid to lose my friends.

In high school, I lied about the psychosis and depression because, as terrifying as it was for me, I didn't want to scare my friends. The more outrageous I was, the more people believed that I was "crazy" in that funny way, which kept the actual mental illness hidden. Protected.

As my life has unfolded, I have lied about so much, thinking that it was the only way I could survive. Survival lying.

If I lie, they'll stay (which never actually worked...they left anyway).

If I lie, they won't get angry at me.

If I lie, they'll never know the truth about me (the sadness, the darkness, the scary stuff that scares me and will definitely scare them).

If I lie, I won't get *as* hurt when they inevitably leave.

If I lie, I stay safe.

If I lie, I keep The Knights at bay (if I hurt myself, they don't have to hurt me).

It's just...I don't want to lie anymore. OK. Now things get really scary.

Time (part ii)

There's a song from the early 1980s that has lyrics that say, "Time/flowing like a river..."

I was pondering that idea the other day. It carries such a peaceful feeling to it: flowing like a river. That has not always been my experience.

Most often, it feels more like time crashing over me! Like a relentless series of waves coming in while trying to find my feet in the chilly Pacific Ocean.

Time has always freaked me out a little bit. Even as a child. And now, as an adult, as a person living in the last half of her fifties, as a never-married woman, as someone owned by an aging dog, as a friend who has lost too many cherished friends to death way sooner than expected, as a daughter whose father died very young (and has now outlived him) and who is witnessing the aging of her mother....as all of these people that I am, I am feeling the sense of time more as a looming specter than a companion on the path.

Time can also be persnickety. There are days when it feels like I have so much time, it moves so slowly and I am surprised to discover how much time I "have."

Then, there are those other days – no time to do anything, feeling rushed, stressed, flummoxed by the lack of time, envious of those days when it feels like there's more than enough time for everything.

And then, there's nap time. Which is a whole other animal! Nap time is like Twilight Zone time.

There are:

the accidental naps. Those are the ones where I'm reading or watching something and then, suddenly, I'm waking up, never realizing that I actually fell asleep.

the intentional naps. When Maddie (the little brown dog) and I choose to lie down and let ourselves just rest, enjoying the sweetness of the daylight streaming in through the windows.

the purposeful naps. Practical, necessary, timed with an alarm.

Regardless of the kind of nap it is, it still becomes lost time. Time that just seems to slip through the fingers, with nothing to show for it.

As with all things, I am Grateful for time. Grateful for memories of happy times, the sting of sad times, the rejuvenation of quiet time, the pleasure of shared time. I suppose time does flow like a river. Sometimes. For me, it also dances and splashes, roars and rages, quiets and stills, and even – on occasion – stops.

And, again, the layers peel away.

Time can stop in a most beautiful way: that first kiss, the moment before opening the award envelope, moments of celebration and connection, the sweet moment of love shared before someone leaves.

And it can feel stopped in deeply painful ways: that last kiss, the moment of not being chosen, the shocking moment of horrible news, the moment after someone is gone.

Time gifts us with beautiful opportunities. And time takes beautiful opportunities from us. It gives us cherished moments and can sometimes leave us with bitter memories.

Time is, in its very essence, a trip!

Looking at photos from the last fifty-plus years of my life, I joke that I can tell how old I am in each photo by my hairstyle. Time told through the choices I made with my hair.

My life has become like chapters in a surreal and bizarre road trip story. There are times in my life when, as I look back, I can't believe that was me! Who WAS that girl?!?

Time is, ultimately, a teacher. It teaches patience, first and foremost. The lyrics of another brilliant song come to mind: "The waiting is the hardest part."

It also teaches wisdom, kindness, perspective, perseverance, and courage.

So...does it flow like a river? Okay. Maybe. If that river has moods, I suppose.

Yeah. I can go with that. I'll sing along with that song now and just insert new lyrics:

"Time/flowing like a river (with moods)..."

Talons

There was a time, back in what I call my "old days," when the depression would come on like a demon. Like many demons. Looking like giant obsidian birds: slimy, dark, with eyes that could terrify the strongest of warriors, sharp talons that dug into my shoulders, my head...That was the pain of the depression. Their talons. With those talons they claimed me. They owned me.

Days when the demons come swooping in, full force, don't happen often (thank goodness). More often than not, they happen when least expected. Which, once again, is a reminder me that depression is never really gone. It's not something I will "get over." It's a thing I have lived with. Will always live with. The worst roommate ever.

Sometimes, the depression comes on like water. Like a gentle tsunami (if such a thing as a gentle tsunami exists).

Like sinking down into a tub of warm water. Almost comforting in its familiarity. And yet, still dangerous if I surrender to it entirely.

Sometimes it shows up like a creeping darkness. Slowly, barely noticeable. Out of the corner of my eye, like seeing my shadow or a bug, I can spot it coming on. And then, I sit down...for hours...as it moves up and over me.

With the demons, as I used to call them - and I will call them out today as what they are - it is all about pain. Just pain. Sharp pain.

Physical, yes. And deeper than that.

Pain that makes it hard to take a deep breath.
Pain that makes sitting uncomfortable.

Pain that makes lying down a bit terrifying.
Pain that makes it nearly impossible to move.

Pain. Internal. External. In my body, my mind, my heart,
my soul.

No reason for it.
No precipitating factor.
No instigator.

Nothing. Just, suddenly....they're there, the demons....
Leering at me, their yellow teeth bared, eyes flashing,
talons out....

If I write about them, write about this moment, it shakes
them, confuses them.

Because to write about them means I am shining light on
them.

Light scares them. Exposes them for the lie that they are.

And, with the dwindling energy I can muster within me, I
say to them the most powerful warrior words I am able to
grasp, offered up by Glinda:

"You have no power here. Be gone. Before somebody drops a house on you."

Eye of the Storm

Recently, I was supporting a friend as she navigated through a difficult time. What came to me was the visual of the eye of the storm.

In a whirlwind, there is a center place of stillness, of quiet, of calm, of seeming nothingness. All around, one step to the side of that center, is complete chaos. Things get whipped around, thrown and tossed, destroyed. Not in the center, though. Not in the eye of the storm.

In the past few days, I have felt thrown and tossed by life. I have witnessed myself engaging in arguments and succumbing to frustration and aggravation. I have lost my self a few times. I have forgotten who I am a few times. And, this has led me into a dangerous place: The darkness. A place I know well.

My favorite movie of all time is *The Wizard of Oz*.

When Dorothy and Toto get swept up into the twister,

the house spins and is lifted off of the ground. When she is in the eye of the cyclone, she has visions. Mostly fun stuff: the two guys fishing, the cow. And then, she has the vision of the one thing that means danger for her: the witch.

As I sit, right now, remembering to pull myself out from the swirling chaos and back into the eye, where stillness is, I am greeted by what could be both my nemesis and my greatest teacher. The darkness. The thing that threatens me, frightens me, forces me to grow, never leaves, and always brings me something that I did not know I needed.

In the film (and book) *Life of Pi*, there is a scene when a terrible storm blows in, quickly and ferociously. It knocks Pi out of his lifeboat. It tosses the little boat around like it is a toy in a bathtub. And Pi notices that Richard Parker, the tiger, is terrified by what is happening.

In the film version of this scene, Pi begins to scream at God. He lets loose at God, "You've taken everything from me! Why are you scaring him?!?"

This always moves me because, in the midst of my own storms, I sometimes get lost in my yelling. It seems necessary to do it. Still, it doesn't seem to really help. I do it anyway because, honestly, it just sometimes feels good to do it. It's just not where I can stay if I want to find someplace to put my feet. To ground my self.

When I was in Assisi, there was a beautiful day that became a stormy day within just a few moments.

I was able to find joy in the storm because I remembered how Brother Francesco used to sing, cry, laugh, and pray during the rain. Sister Water, he called it. I name it the eye of the storm.

I am always at choice as to where I want to stand when I am in the storm.

The chaos, the noise, the flurry of activity that is in the swirling storm around me can cause damage to me, that is true. However, it is also a really great place to hide from the Truth that is in the eye.

The stillness, peace, calm, and safety that is in the eye can bring me back to my True Self, that is true. However, it is also a great place to hide from the chaos and activity in the world.

And, yet (there is always an "and yet," isn't there?), the eye of the storm is the only safe place for me.

To be able to stand on solid ground. To find my feet. To breathe slowly and deeply. To let tears flow. To accept what I am feeling. To know that whatever I am feeling will pass. To be present for my self so that I can be present for others. To do the work I am here to do.

I must stand in the eye of the storm. Stand still there.

Until the storm passes.

Before the next one begins.

Ancora Imparo

As long as I am alive, I am always still learning.

Michelangelo said that: "I am still learning" ("*Ancora imparo*"). They were, in fact, his final words. Which, when you think about it, is pretty amazing.

The man who gave the world so much art – including and

especially the *David* – still felt, as he was leaving the planet, that he was still learning.

On even my worst days, when I feel like I have slid back way more than a few steps (without that one step forward happening at all), I remind myself that as long as I woke up today, I am still learning.

An example I have used in the past about staying open to opportunity is the idea that we cannot catch a ball being tossed in our direction if our fist is closed. Or if we are still holding on to the previous ball that we already caught. We have to have an open hand.

We have to let go of what we are holding on to so that we can receive more Good, more Life, more whatever.

We cannot feel fully free until we let loose the grip.

Rafting in the Grand Canyon, I was – most of the time – filled with terror! I gripped the ropes on the side of that oar boat so tight, I often lost feeling in my fingers. And I could not enjoy the feeling of riding the rapids because I was gripping so tightly.

When I was able to trust, to breathe, to risk, to loosen my grip (just a bit), I ended up having a really fun time! I got splashed, I got knocked around a little bit, I felt free to experience what was happening with an almost complete surrender.

There are times when it's hard to let go. Places we live, people we love, relationships we want, work we feel we need, furry companions we rely on, food we find comfort in, habits we hide behind...ways we live that we have come to accept as "our way." Letting go is not as easy as it sounds.

And yet, how can we receive more Good with our fists closed and clenched, with our hands full of our past?

Every time I have released, let loose the grip, I think, "I've done it! I've let go! I've learned!"...Until the next time.

My Beloved Michael wrote: "So we live and we learn. But we only learn if we live."

Michelangelo, Michael, and me...still learning. As long as we are alive, we are all still learning. *Ancora imparo.*

Goo Time

One of my favorite movies is *Harold and Maude*, for so many reasons.

One of the sweetest moments in the film is when Maude tells Harold, "I like to watch things grow. They grow and bloom and fade and die and change into something else! Ah life!"

Such an inspiring message. As someone who didn't birth or raise children, I have had the pleasure of watching other children grow: nieces, nephews, children of friends. As well as watching my sisters and my mom grow. And friends. And students and young people I have worked with. And, of course, myself. I have watched myself grow.

Going in and out of periodic "Goo Times" – those in-between times when the caterpillar I was wasn't quite ready to emerge as the moth (or butterfly) I was set to become – those are the deepest and most powerful times of growth. Mostly because there is nothing to be done during those times. I just have to sit in the goo, quietly, patiently, reflectively, prayerfully, and wait. If I try to "do" something before I am fully ready, I will make a mess of it. Guaranteed. Goo Time is about actively waiting. Goo Time is essential for growth.

Another metaphor for Goo Time is this: If we plant a seed in the ground, we cannot keep digging it up to "check on it" to see how it's growing. No. We plant, we water, we nurture, and we wait. It's not that nothing is happening or that we have to make something happen to prove we are "doing" something. Growth happens when we wait. Sometimes it's hard to remember that growth is happening while we are waiting.

Goo Times, or Growth Times, don't just happen once in our lives; they happen every time there is change, every time we find ourselves in a new situation, place, moment, "opportunity" (as some like to call it). They happen whenever we realize that we cannot be who and what we were and yet we are not quite ready to become who and what we need to be for this next moment.

Goo Time, like a seed's Growth Time, is safe, quiet, and has no time limit. I used to be afraid of or impatient with Goo Time. Now, I love being in there, in my cocoon, as I wait and rest and Listen. I know that I will Know when it is time to emerge. I continually remind myself that if I try to push or rush it, I won't have the strength I'll need to face what comes next. I've learned that lesson the hard way. The darkness grows the seed.

Goo Time creates the moth or butterfly.

I need to be patient. I need to let myself be gooey, to be a seed in the darkness, to sit in the quiet.

Indeed, Maude. "Ah, Life."

Walking the Switchbacks

It's a strange and kind of surreal phenomenon, this discovery that in my current state of brokenness, I am actually the healthiest I have ever been.

That while facing the darkness, living in it, breathing with it, immersed in it, I still continue to walk through it. It's the semicolon, not the period, in this latest sentence of my life.

I am walking up the switchbacks, moving slowly up from the depths of the abyss.

And it's okay to be scared. It's okay to look back down at where I have come from. It's just about continuing to move forward. Trusting. Making slow progress.

Like walking up Mount Subasio from Assisi. Those switchbacks became the biggest challenge to me. I kept thinking we had reached the top and became frustrated when it was yet another turn to yet another upward path. Tired, hot, thirsty, and ready to be there, I let those switchbacks become my Knight of the Mirrors, trying to dissuade me from my quest.

And yet, I never stopped. I never gave up.

The switchbacks I am facing now are ones I am most grateful for. They have saved me from sliding so far down into the abyss that I couldn't survive. They keep me from losing myself entirely.

So, I don't mind walking up these switchbacks. At each turn in the path, I say a "Thank You" for their protective way of keeping me alive.

I know the abyss is still there. Finally, now, I understand that it always will be there. It's a part of me, part of my story, part of my journey. It's okay to know that it is still there.

And, in this Now, I will keep walking. Upward. Out from
the abyss. Out of the darkness. Again and again. Each
time, finding my way back to the yellow brick road that is
my life, up here, up above the abyss. In the light, in the
air, in the rain, in the sun, in the fullness of this life.

Grateful. In all of it.

Throw the Ball

My friend Nicole and I were talking about how
sometimes I have a hard time getting up and doing
anything. At all. And how, after hours of my non-
movement, my beautiful canine companion Maddie will
stand at the door and stare at me. Relentlessly. All she
wants is to go outside and chase the ball. This, and this
alone, will make her so very happy. And it only takes
about ten minutes. It's simple.

And yet some days even that simple action takes
everything I've got. Depression is a formidable
opponent.

It is the Knight of the Mirrors throwing back at my face all of the harsh appearances that destroy me. It doesn't reflect Truth, only the appearances that keep the Truth from being seen. The Knight of the Mirrors has one purpose: to destroy dreams, vision, and passion. To shine the light of cruelty – not the light of compassion – on my weaknesses.

If I'm feeling alone? It shines light on every relationship failure and my own inability to accept myself, as is, without trying to be someone or something I'm not. Feeling hurt? It will shine light on everything I have done to cause others to hurt me, proving that I deserved it. Feeling hopeless? It shines light on all of the reasons why I should just give up. Afraid to try? It shines light on all of the reasons why it isn't worth trying. When I beg for mercy? I get none.

The Knight of the Mirrors is the one who says, "There is no way from there to here. Because you will always be the way you are. You will never change. Accept it."

It feels like my every effort to stand is met with a push that knocks me back down, hard, until I finally reach the moment of not making any effort. No strength left. It is simply too hard.

So, what must I do? I must remember that every moment of my life has been a process of getting from there to here. From pain to release. From darkness to light. From the couch to standing up.

I must remember that I have – in whatever moment I am in – a 100% success rate of survival.

And I must get back up and go throw the ball. Even if that is the only thing I do the whole, entire day, I must do that much. More than once if I can manage it.

When I am feeling like there's no point to anything, when I am so down into the darkness that nothing is making sense, when it feels like there is simply nothing to be done, just to sit, cry, and give up...Maddie, in her canine wisdom, knows what I need to do:

Take the five steps to the door, slip on the easy-on shoes, grab a jacket and the ball (both within reach), and take the ten to twelve steps out of the door onto the grass. Throw the ball. She will bring it back. Throw it again. Watch her run at top speed. Watch her leap to catch the ball in midair (her favorite technique). Watch her ears flapping as she runs back. Watch her cleverness as she drops the ball just enough out of reach to force me to take another step to pick it back up. Watch her eyes as she holds her breath in anticipation of my throwing it again. Watch her bliss as she takes off running in anticipation of the first bounce. Watch her simply enjoying herself, focusing on nothing except the ball.

And then, after several throws, runs, catches, and returns, she will decide when it's time to go back inside. She drinks some water and lies down on the couch (or the bed, or floor) and chills out for the next few hours. It's that simple. She's happy. It's all she needed.

She doesn't "process" how she did in the yard, how many throws she didn't catch on the bounce, how fast or slow she ran...none of it. She doesn't see or hear the Knight of the Mirrors. She only knows that she really wanted to run and catch, and she did that. And now, she wants to snuggle and nap.

There are some days when I cannot even do this much. My body feels like it's filled with cement. I can barely convince myself to take care of my own basic needs. The "why bother" blanket wraps itself around me, and I can't move. At all.

Knowing that others have it worse than I do doesn't change this experience. Knowing that a good friend is dealing with fighting the battle of life or death, knowing that friends are grieving losses of family members or companion pets, knowing that there are people with so much less than I have...What knowing all of that does is give fuel to the Knight of the Mirrors to show me, reflect to me, prove to me how disgusting and pathetic I am for being this way. Shame on me.

And yet, amazingly, something has changed over the years in the way I experience these worst of days. Something that shifts the energy of self-imposed selfishness and transforms it into something different: Gratitude

Behind and underneath everything is an undercurrent of unwavering gratitude.

I am always grateful for a home, a warm place to be, with my couch and teapot and comfy clothes. Grateful for a mom who understands this experience and is willing to support me and carry me until I can remember how to stand back up. Grateful for friends who possess endless patience and compassion for me as I do battle against the Knight of the Mirrors. Grateful for Maddie, who offers unconditional love, affection, and sweetness (and reminds me to get up and throw the ball). And grateful for so much more, from the little things to the large.

And most of all, I am always grateful for waking up each day. This simple act, that initial moment of awareness that I have woken up again, reminds me that there is a reason for me. There is something for me to do here, in this life. It might be to help a friend. It might be to reach out to someone in deeper darkness than I am. It might be to try something new. It might be to do laundry. It might be to write.

And it might be – simply – to get up and throw the ball.

Surthriving

I like to say that I have earned a master's degree in survival. That is not totally accurate, though.

I have accomplished something more than mere survival.

A spiritual companion gave me a word that describes it much better. This word has become quite useful in my continuing life journey. The word is: Surthrival.

The most important thing we have is right now, this moment.

And even that has already passed.

If I could leave you with any words of guidance it would be these:

Whenever possible, feel Grateful. For clean water. For a cool breeze. For comfortable socks. For music (or silence). For technology (and the freedom to step away from it). For your family (biological or chosen, for better or worse, for all that they have taught you).

Find something - try for three things - each day to be Grateful for.

Even during the darkest times of my life, when I have taken a moment to remember Gratitude, well, that is how I have gotten from each "there" to the next "here." Grateful, in the darkness and in the light.

From there to here. Today. Each day. Again and again.

See you on the journey.

Boundless *Gratitude for those who've helped me grow:*

Mom
Joanie
Nicole
Patrick
Maddie
A.F.
Sarah L, Tracy S, Geri S. and Georgie J.

And, Victoria, who always showed up, pushing every button I had, encouraging and witnessing my growth, continuously reminding me of who I am. Thank you for dragging me to the edge and then watching and celebrating as I learned to fly. Thank you for "Surthrivor". Thank you for making this book a reality.

Even More Acknowledgments:

Celia Lewis, Anita Hollander, Lisa Hollander – sisters who are friends.

All of those patient readers coaches, and editors, most especially Dina Rubin and Lisa Dalton, Thank you

The many friends who have supported me over all of the years – then and now.

The Morning Text Ministry crew.

Thank you, Allison (All-Is-One) for our conversations that started me on this path. (I still have the recording.)

A lifetime of Gratitude for all the Healers, Artists, and Creators who filled me with inspiration to stay here, to never give up, to create, and to face darkness.

My One Spirit Family (most especially, Reverends Diane Berke and David Wallace), My Alaska Circle of women, Spiritual Supports, and Magnificent friends. My Cleveland Circle of Friends. My San Francisco and Boise Circle of friends and ALL of the wonderful ministers and various clergy members who helped me grow.

There are so many people to Thank! Please know that I am Grateful for every one of you!

To H.H. for Maddie.

Acknowledgements
The Songs, Artists, and Films That Tell My Story
(a small sampling)

Duncan Sheik: *Reasons for Living, The Dawn's Request, Those You've Known*

Todd Rundgren: *If I Have to be Alone* and so many more

Judie Tzuke: *Lifeline*

Aquilo: *Human*

Lamb: *Wise Enough*

Movies: *Wizard of Oz, Harold and Maude, Brother Sun Sister Moon, The Poseidon Adventure, Magnolia*

Artists: Vincent van Gogh, Rene Magritte. Miguel de Cervantes, Terry Gilliam